Medieval Dynasty

THE OFFICIAL GUIDE

Publishing company:
BILDNER Verlag GmbH
Bahnhofstraße 8
94032 Passau

http://www.bildner-verlag.de
info@bildner-verlag.de

Author Game Guide: Andreas Zintzsch
Author Chapter-Story: Ivan Ertlov

Translation: Anne-Sophie Hardouin, William Davies

Publisher: Christian Bildner

Special thanks to:
Teresa Steidele, Xhyla Musliu and Martin Donaubauer

© 2022 BILDNER Verlag GmbH Passau

edieval Dynasty surprised in September 2020 as an early access game with a successful combination of several genres and quickly found many enthusiastic players. The game convinced numerous fans visually and with its content, leaving them waiting with high expectations for new features in the updates.

One year later, in September 2021, there was finally the long-awaited full release of version 1.0, which brought outlaws, herbal potions as new features and told a completely new story.

We accompanied Medieval Dynasty through its creation process. A game that would enthrall many gamers was created thanks to the experience of the programmer team from Render Cube and the game enthusiasts from Publisher Toplitz Productions. We would like to thank them at this point for the good cooperation and are pleased to present the official guide of Medieval Dynasty.

Thanks to the stories of best selling author Ivan Ertlov at the beginning of each chapter, the medieval world of our protagonist Racimir seems even more realistic.

As a combination of RPG, survival, crafting, simulation and much more Medieval Dynasty is filled to the brim with interesting and sometimes challenging content. Our practical little reference book will hopefully make the first steps in the game easier for beginners and help more advanced players keep an overview anytime.

Ingame screenshots may be from different game versions, but the information and values have been updated

to the latest version 1.4.1.3 from October 2022. All the information comes from the Steam version on PC but all the available versions of the game, inculding console versions, are identical.

New features and updates will continue to be added to the game after its full release in order to fix eventual bugs and to improve the game experience. That's why some information of the book could later slightly differ from the situations in the game (e.g., if the prices of the goods are adjusted in an update to improve the game balance.)

> In this book, important or interesting hints and information appear in boxes like this one.

Commands, icons, buttons or names of important people or objects are emphasized with colored text, e.g., the village **Gostovia**, the tool **Iron Hoe** or the display screen for **Skills**.

Also, you can find some hints and Let's Play videos about the game on our German speaking Youtube channel Bildner.TV Gaming or on the website **gaming.bildner.tv**

And now, we wish you lots of fun with the game and the book.

The authors and the team of BILDNER Verlag

TABLE OF CONTENTS

TABLE OF CONTENTS

1 Basics

ell, since I am old and grey now, I have decided to tell the posterity how I fared, here in the North, in my new home. The industrious spring passed by ever so fast as did the summer, before autumn commenced with a rich harvest and moved on to the first night frosts and snowflakes of winter. It's strange how time passes by here in the valley. Sometimes, it really seems to fly by, then to almost stand still, to stop for a moment, appreciating the beauty of nature and the fertility of the soil with absolute, divine silence.

I might have become old and frail and, for quite some time now, I do not need to till my fields myself anymore, but this is not a justification for indolence, is it now? There is always something to be done and my hands can still be of good use, even if they are trembling stronger during cold nights than they did one or two years ago. Two weeks ago, I taught archery to my youngest descendant's sprout, simply delightful! But his mother, as stubborn as her father - yes that would be me - thought it was too early for him to learn, but let me tell you, no one is too young to wield a hammer, a bow or a plough!

It's strange how easily the words flow from my quill, I must pay attention, not to smudge the ink of my previous words. Writing? Yes, who would have thought that I would learn this fine art one day, painting words and numbers as once only the harbor masters at the sea in the South did. As far as I know, I am the only one in the valley who mastered it - at least as long until I pass it on to my children, when their offspring shoulder the lion's share of working the fields.

Month after month, I traveled to the neighboring valley, traversing the old, perilous pass in the valley, to visit Edgar, who, by his voluminous belly, is easily recognized as the abbot of the monastery they carved into the mountain there. As a sign of my gratitude I had to deliver to him many pots of honey and even more jugs of honey mead. But it was worth it! A new world opened up to my old eyes and I can leave something for posterity, that may outlast the houses I built in the valley.

Yes, I know that many of my friends don't trust the monks, particularly the ones still nurturing the old faith, who lay their sacrifice bowls on trembling stones, when the moon is full or who visit the shrine of their ancestors in the forest. I can't blame them! But, entre nous, the monks are not that bad, even if the breath of their ink probably rises to their heads in the dark rooms and makes them see some curious things. I should probably avoid this myself, don't you think?

Yes, it's time for me to get up from my writing desk, but not only because of that. Someone just knocked on my door – but I'm not awaiting any visitor any more today. Not this late in the evening...

1 Basics

1.1 The Game and the Main Menu

In Medieval Dynasty you play as the 18 year old character *Racimir*, who flees to a unknown valley to build up a new life there. First, you have to survive in order to progressively build a village, get married and to create a dynasty. The game is a combination of many game genres:

Survival: You have to eat and drink, so you don't starve to death or die of thirst. You get food through hunting, gathering, farming or cattle breeding. Alternatively, you can buy some food from the vendors, but you have to earn your own money before. Getting poisoned, aggressive animals and bandits complicate your survival.

RPG: Like in any typical role playing game, you have to complete some quests and tasks for your fellow inhabitants of the valley and for the king of the country, who sends a herald from time to time. Depending of the task, you can win or lose objects, money, experience and prestige (dynasty reputation).

Crafting: You can craft all the available tools, weapons and objects by yourself. You can also assign a specific job to your village inhabitants, so that they craft objects for you, provided that you give them the required resources.

Build: You can build houses, production facilities, stables and storehouses, compile roads and a lot of decoration, e.g., fences, lamps or tables. Whether you build a small farm at the edge of the forest, a mine estate near a cave in the mountains, a big village with extensive fields or build all these buildings together is up to you.

Simulation: The more prestige (dynasty reputation) you get, the more inhabitants you can invite to your village. You have to provide them with a house and a profession and pay attention to their basic needs like food, water and firewood. You have to react to events in your village (e.g., if a mother can't work the first two years of her child's life) and expand as well as take care of your little community.

Time and Place of the Story

The game takes place around 1000 A.D. in medieval Europe. The exact location isn't given, but there are some vague hints:

You play in a valley with a river and a lake in Eastern Europe, probably in the Polish-Lithuanian region. Not only the names of the villages, of the villagers and of the king indicate that, but also the wild animals you encounter are typical for this region.

You will search for knights, castles, monasteries, churches, priests, monks and big cities in vain. In fact, this would be atypical for medieval Central Europe. Poland only became Christian 966 A.D. and Lithuania even later than that. So, the Christianization of this region did not happen long ago in this game and that's why there doesn't seem to be a single church in this remote valley. The pagan beliefs still remain there. At the wedding ceremony in the game the proceedings are held by a priest, but it is not obvious which religion he practices and this is also not relevant to the game. Unlike in Western and Central Europe, not a lot of castles existed in Eastern Europe.

Probably in the year 1000 A.D. Boleslow I. the Brave of the House of the Piasts became the first polish King.

Goal of the Game

First you have to survive as the 18 years old Racimir and build up a new existence for yourself. Subsequently, you win prestige year after year and recruit inhabitants and workers for your village or your farm. You will look for a wife and have children, thus receiving your longingly awaited heir.

Because the game is inspired by the patriarchal structures of the High Middle Ages, the protagonist Racimir is male and his first heir will be as well. This heir will be the character you will be able to continue the game with afterwards. Currently, it is not possible to play as a female character.

By his 60's at the latest Racimir will die a natural death and you will be able to play as his son, provided that he has already turned 18. Villagers will likewise die but, thanks to their children and new villagers, your village will continue to grow.

There is no final or predetermined ending in this sandbox game. You are supposed to establish your own dynasty and build the village or estate of your medieval dream, no matter how big and powerful or small and cute you want it to be.

With the default settings, one year in the game has 4 seasons with 3 days each. One twelve hour day (without night time) is 24 minutes long in real life. Since you can play with a player character for about 40-50 years, this gives you more than enough time to build your dream village. By then, your son will probably have grown up and you can continue playing with him. Perhaps then the time will be ripe to begin a new game and erect your village at a new place on the map and completely redesign it.

The Main Screen

After starting the game, you see the following menu:

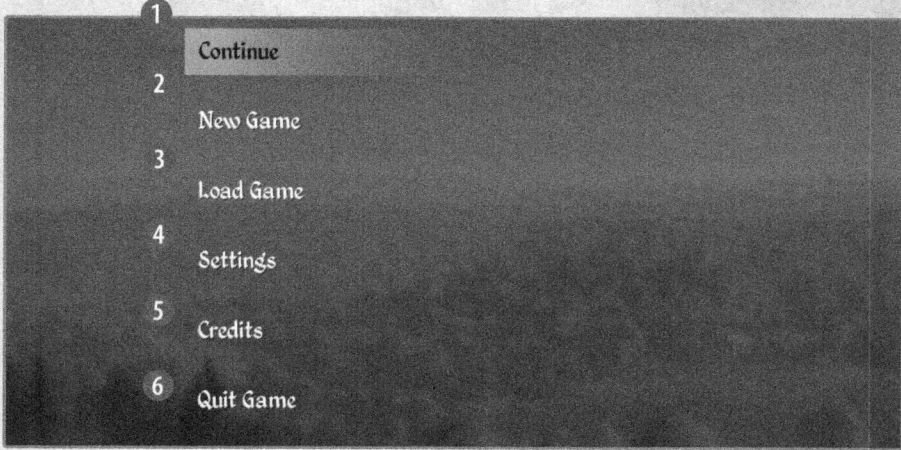

1. **Continue:** loads the latest game state and your game continues from where you last stopped. Only available if at least one saved game exists.

2. **New Game:** you start and choose the settings of a new game.

3. **Load Game:** here you can find all the games you saved and can load or delete one.

4. **Settings:** here you find all the settings for graphics, sound and the keyboard assignments.

5. **Credits:** you see the closing credits of the game and all the people who participated in its creation.

6. **Quit Game:** the game is ended and closed.

1.2   Start a New Game

To start a new game, select *New Game* on the main screen. You should check your *Settings* before beginning to play.

Settings

In the settings, you can adjust the following options:

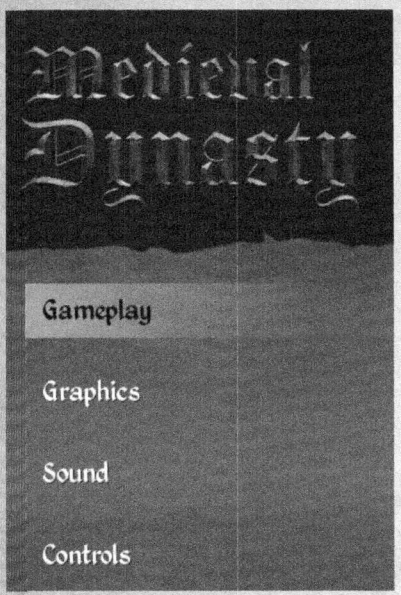

Gameplay

With *Gameplay* you can change the language of the game and the settings of the mouse.

You can also decide, whether you want to see blood or not. The movement of your head when walking can also be turned on and off here.

Another important setting is the interval between every auto-save. By default, it is set to 30 minutes and after each fulfilled quest.

Graphic settings

The graphic settings influence how fluid the game runs. If the game lags, you should lower a few options.

Some settings are explained here:

Window mode: the game looks best when set to *Fullscreen*. You should use *Windowed Fullscreen*, if you want to use other applications often while playing. This mode can, however, create some graphic bugs (rare). The *Windowed* mode only makes sense, if you use a lower resolution, than the resolution you have in Windows. The game will then appear smaller in a window.

Resolution: to have a nice depiction of the game, you should use the highest resolution your monitor offers. If your system is too weak, you can improve the performance by reducing the resolution.

Aspect ratio: currently most monitors use 16:9. Widescreens can display 21:9 or even 32:9.

Field of view: the default view is 90°. If you want to see more on the right and left sides, increase this option. A larger field of view helps players with motion sickness.

V-Sync: adjusts the FPS (frames per second) to the screen refresh rate of your monitor and provides a more fluid picture. Using this only makes sense if the graphic performance of your computer is good enough for the FPS to reach that value constantly.

View distance: determines how far you can see. The further you can see, the more your computer has to calculate. Set this parameter down if the game lags.

Foliage: the representation of foliage and grass is, of course, beautiful but consumes a lot of computer power. You could save a bit of power by lowering this setting.

All other settings: strongly depend on the graphic card you use. With a newer and more powerful graphic card you can increase these settings. Try adjusting these options to find the best settings allowing a fluid gameplay.

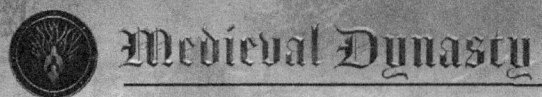

Medieval Dynasty

Sound settings

With *Sound*, you can change the volume of all single elements.

Controls

In this book, we use the game's default settings for PC and controller controls for the explanations. But you can, of course, change the key assignment for each letter of every key and set up an alternative PC key mapping that you can use in parallel with the default mapping. To do this, *double-click* on an entry with the *left mouse button* and press the *desired key*.

> Don't forget to save changes with *C* / Ⓨ / Ⓐ ! With *X* / Ⓧ / Ⓑ, you can reset the keyboard settings.

Customize the Game

When you start a new game, you can choose the rules for it under *Customize Game*:

Most of these settings are self-explanatory, you can, for example, turn the ability of your character to have unlimited life or stamina on or off. With a slide bar you can also determine the health points of animals and the amount of experience you receive. The further right you drag the slider control with your right mouse button, the higher these values will be.

> The default values are optimized from the game developers for having an exciting game with all facets optimized. For your first game, we recommend using the default settings!

If you want more of a challenge, you can increase the setting of the *Taxes* (you'll have to pay more taxes, 200% means twice as many taxes as the default settings at the beginning of each new year!), the *Health Points* and *Damage* of your enemies (animals and bandits) and the *Needs* of your inhabitants.

If you only want to build a lot and use less of the other elements of the game, then activate *Unlimited Carry Weight*, *HP* and *Stamina* as well as *Lack of Hunger* and *Thirst* and also *Fast Crafting*. Put all *Experience Multipliers* and the *Buildings Limit* on maximum and the *Needs* of your inhabitants to minimum. Also activate *Stop dropped Items from Spoiling* if you want to decorate your village with food.

Length of Season (days)

A season normally lasts 3 days. This is the optimal setting. Consider that increasing this also means you require more resources, like food, and more time for many things (e.g., the time between sowing and harvest).

1.3   Using a Controller

In this guide we will give you the info and tips based on the controls for PC / Xbox / PlayStation. Of course, you can also use controllers on the PC. Here are the most important settings.

Controller settings

To set up the controller, you need to select *Controls* in the settings.

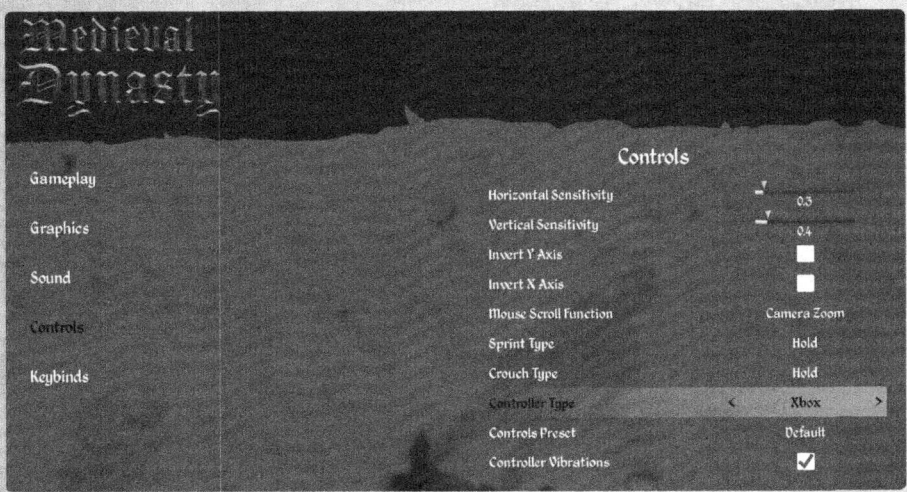

Then select your controller under *Controller Type* and apply these settings. There are 4 predefined control combinations that you can select under *Controls Preset*. You can then see the controls of the selected combination under *Keybinds*.

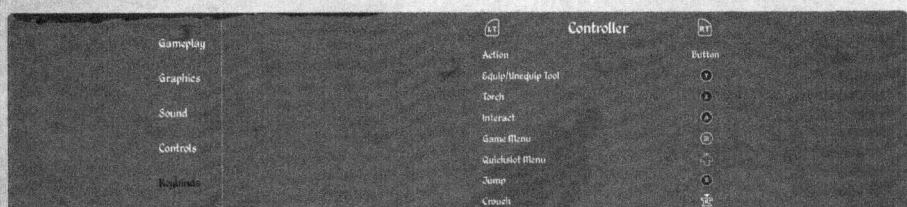

Playing with a controller

In each menu, the keys that can be used are displayed at the bottom right. Use these to navigate through the menu and make settings.

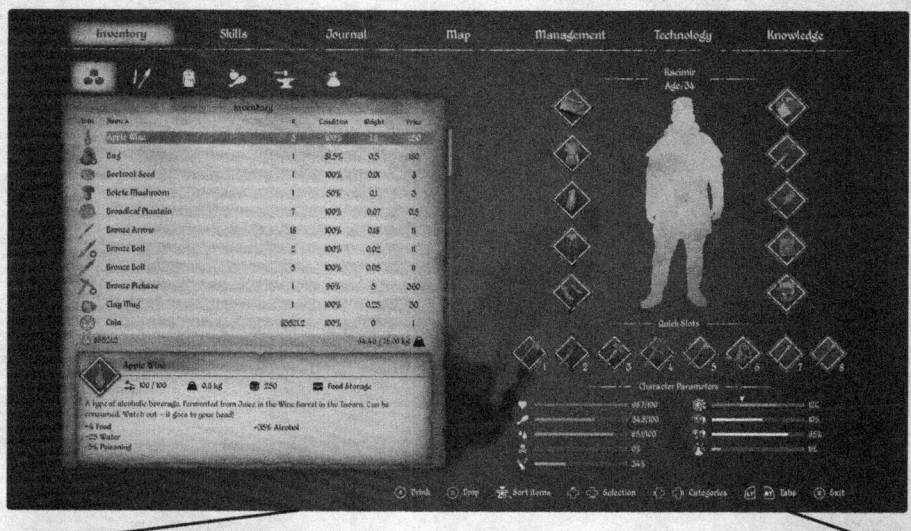

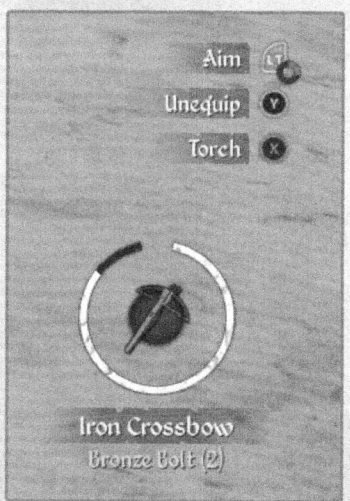

Even the tool display in the lower right part of your HUD shows you the respective controller keys that you can use with the selected tool.

1.4 Gamescreen

When you start the game, you see the gamescreen with the HUD (Head-Up Display) in front of you. The HUD gives you information right on your screen. You can open further windows with different keys, which we present below:

HUD

1 Display of life, stamina and other effects.

2 Your selected tool / weapon.

3 Your tool or weapon with its active state and its name.

4 Your current quest or task.

5 Compass with direction signs and season indication.

6 Warning of supply shortage of your inhabitants.

7 Indications (e.g., lost or received items).

In the bottom left corner, you find a detailed view of your life and other effects:

1 Stamina – regenerates through waiting or walking slowly; a *Potion of Stamina* improves your stamina briefly.

2 Health – regenerates through sleeping, healing potions and the consumption of broadleaf plantain.

3 Food – eat something from your inventory.

4 Water – drink from lakes, rivers or from beverages or eat berries and soups.

5 Dirtiness – climb into a lake or a river or wash yourself at a washtub.

6 Overburdened – throw objects away, use backpacks, pouches or the *Potion of Weight*.

7 Temperature - change your clothes depending on the seasons or drink a potion of temperature.

8 Alcohol – drink an alcohol potion. Vanishes after some time.

9 Poison – use *Cure Potion* or eat St. John's Wort. Heals overtime.

Tool Display

In the bottom right corner, you see your currently selected tool or weapon. You have to assign tools and weapons to keys *1-8* in your inventory. Once done, you can select each tool by pressing the *assigned key on PC* and ⬆/⬇ on the controller.

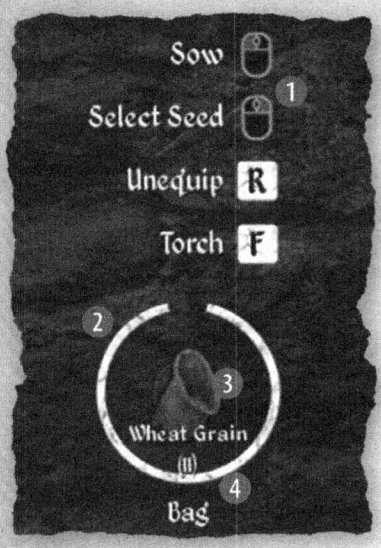

①   Hint of the functions you can use with the tool / weapon you have selected.

②   The white ring shows the condition of your tool. If the ring has completely disappeared, the tool is destroyed. You can't repair tools!

③   The image of the tool. Some tools also show additional information. Here you can see, that you have 11 grains of wheat in your bag.

④   The name of the tool/ weapon.

Key Indications

The key indications that show up in the tool display are very helpful if you're still learning how to use a specific tool. For example, the image above explains that you can select seeds by clicking the *right mouse button* or pressing LT / L2 when using the bag!

The compass

At the top middle of the screen you can see the compass

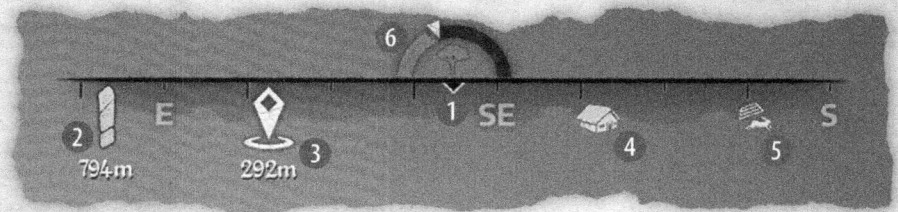

1. The direction you are looking in.

2. A yellow exclamation mark shows you the place you have to go to complete your current quest. Underneath it, you see the distance you have to cover to get there.

3. This icon shows the waypoint you set on the map and how far away it is.

4. The house you live in.

5. One of your nearby animal traps.

6. The season display. Depending on how full the colored bar is, you can see how far the season has advanced.

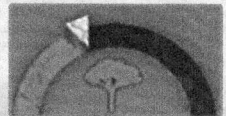   

| Spring | Summer | Autumn | Winter |

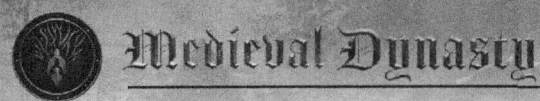

Inventory

With I / ⊚ / Cr , you can open your inventory:

1. In this bar, you can change the inventory displays you see in area 2: all objects, only tools/weapons, clothes, consumables, raw materials and valuable objects.

2. You can see all objects in the inventory with their image, their name, their number, their condition in %, their weight in kg and their price. You can sort all items by these settings: alphabetically, price ascending-descending, etc.

3. Select an object in area 2 to get further information about it: e.g., the exact condition of a tool, the nutritional value of food or the extraction force of a tool.

4. *Double-click* / press the key Ⓐ/Ⓧ on an article of clothing from area 2 and you'll wear it or take it off. When equipped, the item is highlighted with a red circle in the inventory 2 and will be displayed on the left side of your character's silhouette 4 in the corresponding fields.

5 In this area, additional tools like arrows, torches, bagpacks and pouches are shown. They can be equipped and unequipped like clothes.

6 Here, the 8 slots of your equipment bar are indicated. They correspond to the numbers on your keyboard or to the *tool wheel*, that you can open with ⬆/⬆ . Select a tool or weapon in your inventory **2**, then *click* / press Ⓐ/Ⓧ on the desired field. You can also press the keys *1-8* on the PC instead of *clicking* on the desired field. While playing, you can press the keys *1-8* or use the *tool wheel* to equip the corresponding object.

7 Here you can see the statuses that influence your character:

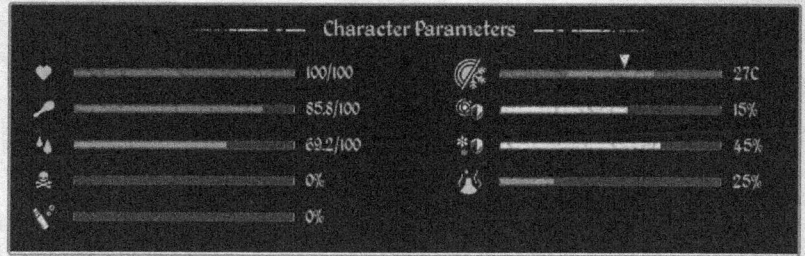

In the left column from top to bottom: Your health points, your food saturation, your level of thirst, your level of intoxication and level of alcoholization.

In the right column: In the right column, the temperature felt by Racimir, including clothing effects, underneath that your heat protection and then your cold protection and at the bottom you see how dirty you are.

Skills

By pressing **K /** 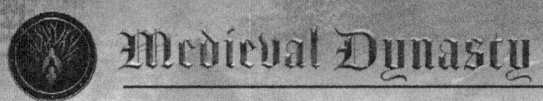 **/ Cr** , you open your skills:

There are 6 different skill trees: *Extraction*, *Hunting*, *Farming*, *Diplomacy*, *Survival* and *Production*. For each action of the skill tree performed, you receive experience correspondingly. When you have enough experience, you get an experience point you can use to unlock another skill, which improves your performance in the respective skill tree.

1 In this bar, you can switch between the 6 different skill trees by choosing one of the icons.

2 Here you can see the number of skill points you can spend.

3 The list of the different skills you can unlock and increase for a skill tree. The color of the icon shows if the skill is already acquired (green), unlocked (gray) or not available yet (black). You also see how many levels you've already unlocked for each skill, the amount of available upgrades (e.g., 2/3) and the level of the skill.

4 If you select a specific skill in area **3** , you can see an exact description of this skill.

5 In this row, you can see how many skill points you can spend, the level of this skill tree (maximum 10) and how much experience you still need until you reach the next level (e.g., 467,5/500). A maximum of 15 skill points can be received and spent in each skill tree.

6 The skill tree: there are 4 levels, rising from the bottom of the tree to its top. You first have to unlock a level 1 skill before being able to unlock a level 2 skill and so on. Select a skill to learn more about it in area **4**. If you want to increase a skill, select an icon in the skill tree or in area **3**.

Some skills can be upgraded 3 times and others only once.

7 In the lower bar, you can see the keyboard commands.

Potion of Possibilities

With a potion of possibilities, all the acquired skills of all skill trees are reset, you regain all the skill points and can spend them again, rearranging them in a new way. This potion will make you drunk.

Journal

Pressing J / ◎ / ⒸⓇ opens the journal.

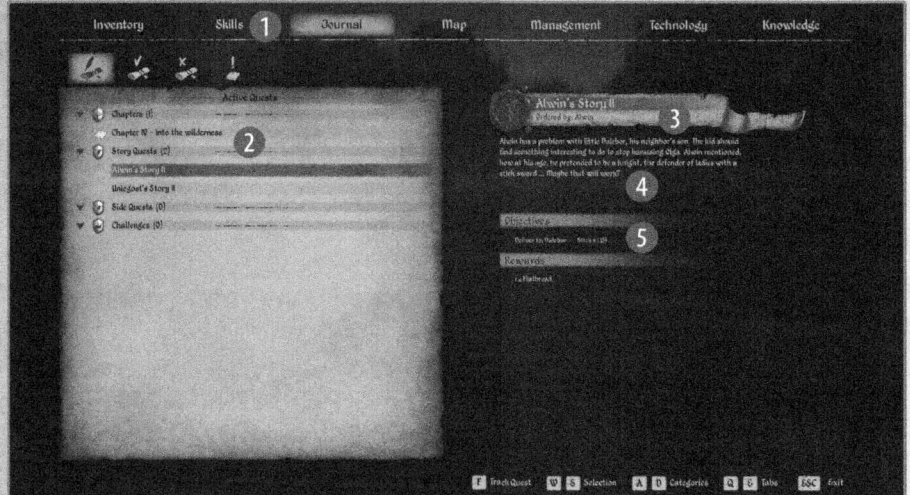

In the journal, you find an overview of all quests and tasks you received so far.

❶ In this row, you can change the overview:

» Active quests

» Completed quests

» Failed quests

» History of recent events

❷ In this area, you have a list of all quests and tasks. You can choose your current quest/task with a *Double-click* / Ⓐ / ⓧ. The active quest will be shown as a yellow exclamation point in the HUD on the compass. Furthermore, the goals of your current quest will be shown at the top right of your screen (see *HUD* point **❹** and **❺**).

Quests and tasks are divided in 4 types:

» **Chapters**: are the most important tasks, which you should do at the beginning. They give you the most dynasty reputation. The number of buildings you can build depends of the chapters.

» **Story Quests**: quests and tasks from specific inhabitants, like for example from Uniegost or Alwin, which tell a story and can extend over years.

» **Side Quests**: you get these quests from random inhabitants of the valley. For each quest, you get different kinds of rewards like skill experience, dynasty reputation, objects or coins.

» **Challenges**: you receive challenges from the Herold of the king, who can randomly appear during a year. When he appears, you recognize and find him by his ceremonial trumpet icon on the compass in the HUD. By successfully completing challenges you gain prestige with the king and receive various rewards. But be careful: if you support a bad king (e.g. Chwalibog I the Greedy or Egon I the Cruel) your reputation with the inhabitants will decrease.

3 When you select a quest in area **2**, an exact description of it appears.

4 The objectives of the quest are clearly listed here again. You also see those you already completed.

5 Here you can see the reward for completing the quest.

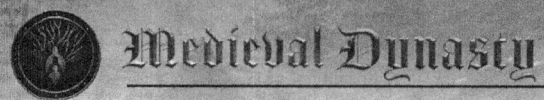
Map

By pressing *M* / ⊚ / Cr , you open the map:

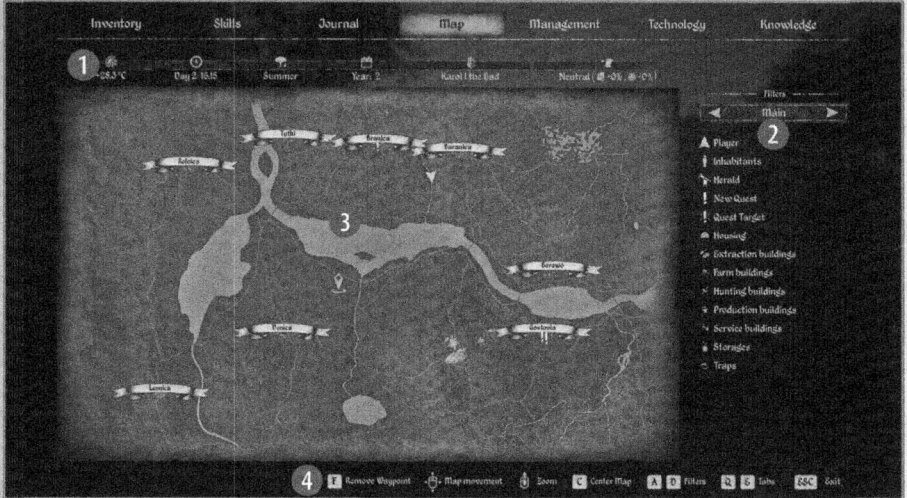

① This information row shows the current temperature, the time, the season, the year, the current king and your reputation with him.

② Use the *arrows* / ◀ ▶ / ◀ ▶ to switch to a different map mode. What it represents is displayed just below it with an icon and text.

③ The map of the valley. The icons on the map are explained on the right side ②.

» Hold down the *Left Mouse Button* and drag it in any direction to move the map.

» Use the *Mouse Wheel* / ↕ ↕ / ↑ ↓ to zoom in/out of the map.

» Point to a place on the map and *Double-click* or press *F* to set a waypoint, which is also displayed on the compass in the HUD.

With a controller you can move with ®/®③ and set the waypoint with Ⓐ/⊗.

» Press **C**/Ⓨ/Ⓐ on the map to center your current position.

④ The most important commands are displayed in this line.

Here you can see the village of Gostovia close up.

You can see:

» 1 active quest (yellow ?)

» 2 potential quest givers (yellow !)

» The herald of the king with a challenge (white ceremonial trumpett 🎺)

» The position of the player and his viewing direction (triangular arrow)

» The waypoint set by the player 🏺

Management

With **N** / ⊚ / ⒸⓇ , you open the management display screen:

With the management screen, you can manage your inhabitants, your houses, your production facilities, your fields and your stables. This window is essential to manage the consumption and production of your village and its inhabitants. For this reason we give a detailed description of the village management in *Chapter 7.2. Village Management*.

🔵 In this line, you can choose between different management windows in area ②: people (person management), buildings, crops (field management), animals and consumption control.

🔵 Here you can see a list of all the objects available in a specific section (e.g., people or houses) with the most important information. *Double-click* or press **F** / Ⓐ / ⓧ on an object, a window with details of the selected object will appear on the right side.

3 The selected object of area **2** will stand out on the map. In addition, you also see the position of your character as a yellow triangle.

4 In this area, you see a lot of information, e.g., how many inhabitants and how much food supplies you have. The numbers in brackets next to food, water and wood indicate how much you need per day to supply your population.

In the opened detail window, you can assign a house or a profession to an inhabitant with a *double-click* /⊗/⊗ **5**. The detailed view is also subdivided into different sectors depending on the selected object. You can select a different sector in the bar at the top **6**.

In the example on the right, you can see the detailed view of a building, a barn level 3. In the bottom part, you can see the assigned workers and the information in detail **5**. By *double-clicking* or pressing ⊗/⊗ on the name, you can adjust and change the worker or assign a new worker.

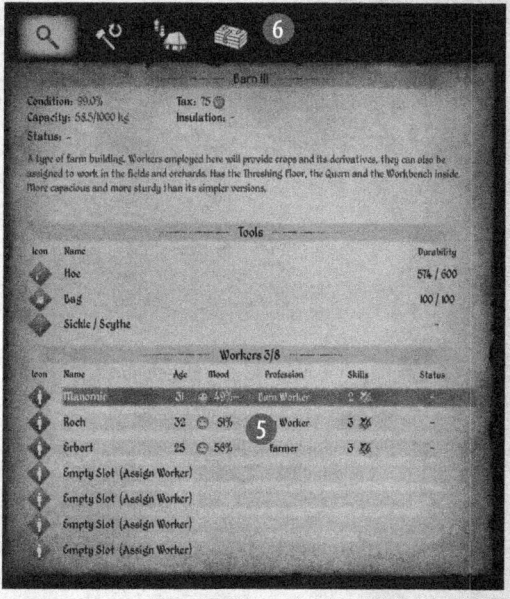

In the other sectors **6**, you can change the objects you want to be crafted and in the third and fourth option, you can see all the objects that have already been crafted and all the objects stored in the building.

Technology

With *T* / ⊚ / Cr , you open the technology display screen:

There are 4 technology sections, in which you can get experience: *Building Technology*, *Surviving Technology*, *Farming Technology* and *Production Technology*. This experience is independent from your skills. E.g., when going hunting, you gain experience for the hunting skill but also in the surviving technology.

1 In this row, you can switch between the 4 technologies.

2 Here you can see the collected experience in the selected technology.

3 All buildings that you can unlock with technology experience are listed from top to bottom. The needed experience to automatically unlock a building is shown at the left side and the green bar shows you how much experience you gathered so far.

4 When selecting a building in area 3, you get further information on it.

Buildings are unlocked automatically, as soon as you gathered enough experience points. However, a lot of buildings provide you with schemes required to craft some objects, which you have to pay for first. Click on a building in area ❸ and all the available schemes will appear, also indicating their price. A green icon means, the scheme has already been acquired. You buy a scheme by *double-clicking* or with a *single click followed by* pressing *F*, provided you have enough coins. Press /Ⓐ/Ⓧ on the controller to buy a scheme.

❺ Here you can see more precise information about a selected house or scheme. Amongst other things, the needed resources to craft a specific object are shown.

Do You Really Need All the Schemes?

You only should buy a scheme, if you really need the object. Particularly at the beginning of the game, when money is still rare, you should consider which objects you want to spend your coins on.

You can, e.g., find (or steel) a bow at the beginning of the game and buy some iron arrows of high quality. In return, you will be able to wait a long time before buying the schemes for arrows or bows since the iron arrows have better durability and are significantly more effective than stone arrows.

Also consider, that you need resources to craft an object and that the scheme alone is useless.

Knowledge

With *L* / ⊛ / Cᵣ , you open the knowledge library:

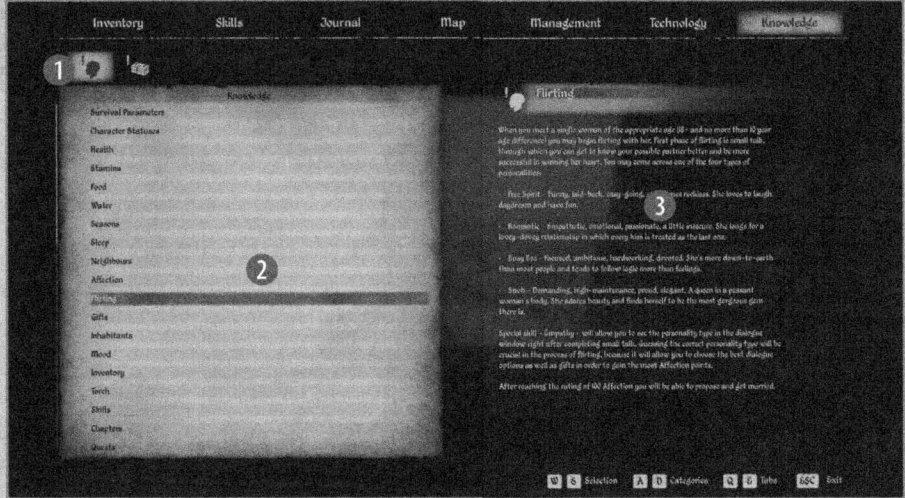

① You can choose between the general knowledge (e.g., flirting, mood, etc.) and the knowledge of resources and objects.

② All the topics are listed in this area. You can move to the top or to the bottom of the page by using the *Mouse Wheel* or the keys *W & S* / ◀✦ ✦▶ / ◀◉ ◉▶ . Choose a topic and you will learn more about it on the right side.

③ All the information of a selected topic is shown here, specifically a more precise explanation about a specific action or the description of tools and resources with details about their crafting price and where to find them. Sometimes, a short video is shown.

1.5 Seasons

The changing of seasons and how it influences the game and the appearance of landscapes is what makes Medieval Dynasty so special: the pale green of spring is replaced in summer by an even richer and juicier green, characterized by dense vegetation and ripe berries. In autumn, many mushrooms sprout in the forest and the trees turn the landscapes gold. In winter snow covers the valley and nothing grows anymore.

With the default settings, a season lasts 3 days. You can adjust this anytime but consider this: fewer days make it more hectic to get everything done in one season, and more days mean more resources are needed and longer waiting times occur (e.g., until the next harvest).

The season changes on the third day at 12 p.m.. You will then be automatically teleported back to your bed and wake up in your house the next day. You don't have a house? Then you will wake up at the firecamp of the nearest village.

Carrying Problems?

On the last day of a season, just before midnight, overload yourself with all the objects you can carry. At midnight, you will be teleported to your house with your complete inventory.

Consequences of the change of seasons

» At 12 p.m., you are teleported to your house and wake up there on the next day.

» Many active quests end with the changing of the season. Be sure to complete all of them before the season changes or they will fail!

» Food loses durability, depending on the place it is stored in and the type of food it is.

» The vegetation changes, there are different plants or mushrooms in the forest (in the winter there are none).

» A lot of resources regenerate: e.g., depleted rock, salt and metal deposits can be mined again and sticks and stones respawn. Tree stumps only grow back after 2 years, and dug up stumps don't regrow at all.

» Random places are newly generated: overturned carts, discarded backpacks; abandoned camps are randomly respawned. You will find objects and resources there. The places where these can appear are fixed, but whether they are generated is coincidental each season. Nothing will respawn near buildings.

» The inventory and the money of vendors get reset to their default values. All objects you sold to the vendors disappear from their inventory. Their default inventory and money is fixed but the amount can still vary to a certain extent.

» New travelers can appear next to the campfires and children can be born in the villages. Animals can also get offspring.

» The herald of the king can turn up in a tavern.

» An event can take place.

» The vendor for exotic goods can be found in a different random village.

Spring

The taxes are due. Pay them to castellan Uniegost in Gostovia or send your wife to pay them. Otherwise, you lose prestige and your debt increase. Your prestige keeps falling until you pay your debts. If your debts become to high or your prestige to low, the game ends.

Gathering of plants:

> Unripe Berries

> Morel Mushroom

> St. John's Wort

> Broadleaf Plantain

> Daisy

> Dandelion

> Chicory

Sowing the fields:

> Wheat (harvest in autumn)

> Oat (harvest in autumn)

> Flax (harvest in summer)

> Carrot (harvest in summer)

> Cabbage (harvest in summer)

> Beetroot (harvest in autumn)

> Onion (harvest in summer)

> Poppy (harvest in autumn)

Harvesting:

> Rye (sowed in autumn)

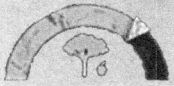

Summer

During harvesting time, you possibly will have to help your farmers with harvesting or the gathering of plants.

Gathering of plants:

> Ripe Berries

> St. John's Wort

> Broadleaf Plantain

> Daisy

> Dandelion

> Thistle

> Chicory

> Henbane

> Deadly Nightshade

Sowing the fields:

> Cabbage (harvest in autumn)

Harvesting:

> Cabbage (sowed in spring)

> Carrots (sowed in winter)

> Wheat (sowed in autumn)

> Flax (sowed in spring)

> Onions (sowed in spring)

> All fruit trees

Medieval Dynasty

Autumn

As preparations for winter continue, gather enough firewood and bring the remaining harvest in.

Gathering of plants:

> St. John's Wort
> Broadleaf Plantain
> Chicory
> Mushroom: Bolete Mushroom
> Mushroom: Bitter Bolete Mushroom
> Mushroom: Parasol Mushroom
> Mushroom: Fly Agaric Mushroom
> Mushroom: Red Pine Mushroom
> Mushroom: Wooly Milkcap Mushroom

Sowing the fields:

> Wheat (harvest in summer)
> Rye (harvest in spring)

Harvesting:

> Wheat (sowed in spring)
> Oat (sowed in spring)
> Carrot (sowed in spring)
> Cabbage (sowed in summer)
> Beetroot (sowed in summer)
> Poppy (sowed in spring)
> Hop

Winter

During fallow time, there is almost no sowing and harvesting. Use this period to hunt and gather other resources and don't forget to put on warm clothes!

Expand your village, complete quests, explore the landscapes – during this season, you have time for many other things.

If you have food problems, you can feed your inhabitants and yourself effectively by hunting.

Gathering of plants:

> None

Sowing the fields:

> Carrot (harvest in summer)

Harvesting:

> None

Medieval Dynasty

1.6 Experiencing the first year

At this point, we want to accompany you through your first hours in the game and give you some hints for the first year:

» You start in the forest. Look to the left, if you're lucky, you will find an overturned cart (random spawn) with a tool and a straw-hat.

» Go north to the village of *Gostovia*. Gather sticks and stones on your way and craft as many stone knives as you can carry. Speak with the castellan Uniegost in Gostovia (as your currently active quest indicated with a yellow exclamation mark on the compass) and get your next chapter quest. Sell all the stone knives you crafted to a vendor in the village.

» Your primary goal from now on should be to complete the chapter quests, as these introduce you to the game. Only by completing the individual chapters will you gain enough dynasty reputation, so that you can build more buildings and thus larger villages.

» Leave Gostovia and head to the east of the map by following the road along the river until you reach a bridge. With a bit of luck, you'll find an overturned cart with a bronze axe in it (random spawn) at the fork with a signpost.

» Look for the flattest place possible to build your house and later your whole village. For your first game, we recommend that you build near a water source and not too far away from Gostovia since you have to go there regularly to pay your debts and accept many quests. There should be reeds in the water nearby, then you don't have to go so far for straw (later you'll also get straw from harvesting your fields).

» Build your first house out of logs, sticks and straw (reed). Your next houses should be made of stone walls with a wooden tile roof, as they are better isolated and consume less firewood! But a small house is sufficient for the beginning.

» Don't go to bed during the night. Rather use the time to collect sticks and stones, in order to craft even more stone knives. Use a torch to see better in the dark. Not sleeping doesn't have any negative effects on you. The only drawback is the darkness.

» After you have built your house and done the chapter quest *A New Beginning*, stow all the unnecessary objects in the chest inside your house. Take all your knives and your money with you and make your way to *Hornica* (alternatively to *Lesnica*). If you pass through another village on the way, sell all the knives you have and continue gathering resources and crafting knives until you arrive.

» You should have some skill points by now. First, always increase the *Skill of Knowledge* for every skill tree. With your second skill point, increase *Survival Sense* in *Survival*. You can now see plants, sticks and stones way better and also see equipment on the ground, e.g., shot arrows or thrown spears, by pressing the *Alt* / LB / L1 key.

» Once arrived in Hornica (or Lesnica), sell all the knives you made and go to the village blacksmith. Buy and equip a *Longbow* and all the *Iron Arrows* he has. These simplify hunting, which will come up a lot from now on. If you still have money or time to craft and sell other knives, you can buy other iron tools. In Hornica, you can also buy *Pouches* or *Backpacks*, which allow you to carry significantly more weight.

» With a single headshot, you can kill animals like deers, wolves and boars. From a safe distance, you can even kill wisents with 2-4 iron arrows. Don't forget that you can look for the shot arrows with the *Alt* / LB / L1 key and retrieve them! If the arrows disappear, they are broken. You should have finished chapter II by now.

» In chapter III, you have to complete several quests. The best thing to do is to go to Uniegost in Gostovia and complete his first quest row. This will lead you to the hermit *Sambor* to the north east of the map.

On your way, you will pass by a broken fence. Next to the cart that crashed there, it is possible you find a *Waterskin* (Random spawn), which you are not yet able to craft by yourself. As a second quest, we recommend to begin the quest row of Alwin in Gostovia. The story quests of Uniegost and Alwin last throughout many chapters and even years. For this reason, you should start with them as early as possible. You have a large period of time to fulfill them but they still expire. As your third quest, we recommend a quest from an inhabitant of a village and to flirt with a woman at a camp fire.

» In the next chapters, you will have to construct several buildings, keep hunting (*Bronze* or *Iron Spears* are expensive, but with 2 you can easily kill any wisent). You also have to recruit your first inhabitants.

» Go to a campfire in a village and press the *Alt* / LB / L1 key, while looking at your potential inhabitants. You will see their skills over their head. The best inhabitants to begin with are hunters and lumberjacks, as you can already construct the buildings for them to work in. Through this, the food and wood needs will be covered.

» You have to build a house for your inhabitants (preferably made of stone) and provide them with food (it does not matter what kind), water (in a waterskin or in a bucket) and firewood. At the beginning, you will have to put all of these things into the respective *Chests* of the houses.

» You must assign villagers to residences (one woman and one man per house) and commercial buildings via the buildings management screen. Depending on the building you have assigned them to, they will begin their corresponding work.

» A *Well* with a water carrier and a *Kitchen* with a cook complete your village supply.

» Build a *Food Storage* and a *Resource Storage* as soon as you can. Then you won't need to put food, water, firewood and tools for the workers into the respective chests anymore. Instead, you can put them into the respective storage. Your inhabitants take the things they need by themselves when they are in the storage facilities.

» Now it's up to you how you continue developing your village. You should have survived the first year without any major problems.

Additional general tips:

» Take your time and don't become hectic because of the seasons. By gathering and hunting, you always find enough food to survive. You don't need to farm a lot at the beginning. Just postpone it if you want to.

» You don't have to build the facilities for all the different professions. A lot of jobs produce enough surplus that you can sell. You can also buy the objects you don't have with that money and don't need to produce them all by yourself.

» Don't make your village too big too quickly. As soon as the first women have children and are no longer available for 2 years due to motherhood, you will have to replace them or fill in for them. If you have too many villagers, it can quickly come to bottlenecks when some workers drop out, which you cannot fix so quickly on your own!

» Look for the right place for your village. At the beginning of the game your village is still small, but keep in mind that you can build up to 65 buildings (130 if the building's limit is set on 200%). If you want to farm with fields and orchards, you'll need quite a bit of space and preferably a lot of flat land!

1.7 Updates

This book was originally written for version 1.0 of the game. Numerous updates have come since then, which have added some new things to the game. In October 2022, the long-awaited console release of the game finally happened. Here's a brief overview of the updates and changes since version 1.0 for PC, so that new players or even old hands returning to the game after a long time of absence can see how the game has evolved.

All values, prices, names and mechanisms described in the book have also been updated and are at the current state of the game version 1.4.1.3 from October 2022.

More game updates with new features will follow. Armor and weapons, and finally a multiplayer co-op mode are planned. The book will continue to be updated with major updates. The next book update is planned for the release of the co-op version in 2023.

Important new features since version 1.0

» Switch the view between *first person* and *third person*. Use the desired key (*Settings - Controls*) to switch, so you can finally see what Racimir is wearing as clothes.

» *Game settings* can now be changed while playing (e.g. duration of seasons, building limits or the occurrence of outlaws). Press the ESC key while playing to get to the menu and select *Customize Game Settings* to change the individual items.

» The *Windmill* has been added as a new building in the *Agriculture* section. It provides an improved grindstone (millstone) and has space for a worker (miller). However, the millstone in the *barn* remains. The mill produces twice the quantity of flour than the barn with the same amount of grain.

» 5 *birds* came into the game as huntable game: *pigeons*, *ducks*, *crows*, *hawks* and *white tailed eagles*. If you kill a bird you get meat and feathers. For a fee, you can have the hunters in Lesnica and Tutki draw the locations of the respective birds on your map. You can also find nests and feathers.

» Over 100 new interesting random spawn locations have been added to the world. Thus, there are now many more abandoned camps, broken-down carts or buried crates to find. There are now so many that it would not make sense to draw these additional locations on the existing maps, as the map would then no longer be legible due to the many symbols. The spawn locations are now automatically added to the map when walking by.

» Likewise, the number of locations of possible outlaw camps has been significantly increased. Again, the map was not adjusted, as it would otherwise become unreadable.

» Defeating bandits now increases the dynasty's reputation.

» Falling trees can harm the player and even knock him out and throw him off his horse.

» In the house construction, another intermediate step has been added: first you can decide where to build the building. This costs you nothing, since you don't need any materials for it. After that, the foundation is built of stone or wood, then the framing, followed by the walls and the roof.

» Living houses can now be furnished outside and inside (e.g. with shelves, candles, lanterns or trophies on the walls, carpets for the floor, curtains for the windows or lanterns and Himmeli for the attic). In addition, there are different shutters and doors to further customize houses.

» It is now also possible to upgrade the modules of other houses (warehouses, factory buildings, such as blacksmiths or work-shops). (e.g. add plaster to the walls once the skill has been learned).

» Donkeys have received their own shelter. This means that you can now buy and shelter the donkey much earlier than a horse. From now on, the horses have the stable exclusively for them-selves.

» A fast travel to other villages is now possible via carts at the villages. The prices for these are balanced so that they are still very expensive at the beginning of the game. This encourages exploration and saves annoying paths in the endgame.

» The family system has been completely reworked. Wife and son now offer family quests where you can get unique new villagers for your settlement.

» Like the player's wife, the son now has a personality as well. The haircut ceremony determines how the boy develops. Education and apprenticeship also take a larger place and determine the further life path of the offspring.

» From the age of 14 all children can be sent to apprenticeship, so they improve their ability in the learned profession.

» Gifting children increases your Dynasty reputation and encour-age them to play.

2 The Valley

h, a visitor? This late in the evening? Well, dear stranger, come in, come in! Make yourself comfortable at the fire and don't hesitate to help yourself to the soup, which is still simmering on the stove! The night will be cold and you look like you could do with some warmth and refreshment. Looking at your face, you come from the South, don't you? The color of your skin made it clear to me, only the people down by the ocean have such a bronze complexion. But, like mine, it will fade over time. Because, let me tell you a secret: I too once came the long way north, alone, starving, freezing and poor as a beggar in these city streets! But everything has turned out better. Well, almost everything. My real life only began as I walked into this valley.

I remember it as if it was yesterday. The last steps I made over the mountain pass, I should better say staggered ! Tired and hungry, still half frozen from the cold nights in the Alps, I had to cross to get here. Marked by the horrors of the war, which drove me out of my home town. Can you see this scar on my left arm? No, it wasn't a soldier, who burnt down my childhood home, my family...

... excuse me, we don't want to talk about such dark things, do we? No, I have to thank a bandit for this scar. On a dark forest path between the Danube and Prague, he took my last belongings from me. But wait, he wasn't satisfied with that. He wanted to take *my life, probably so I could not tell the city thugs in the next village what happened to me. But, as you see, he did not get it! Believe me when I say, I beat him up worse than he did me. But he got away with the few copper coins and the last silver piece I had.*

Where was I again? Oh, right, my arrival into the valley as a stranger, searching for a new beginning, a future, a home and a hearth. At that time, this dream seemed to me as beautiful as the valley itself. I ran down the hill and couldn't believe my eyes as I saw this idyll! The river, glittering in the sunlight. Dense forests with strong and healthy trees providing wood for the houses and the farms. And the villages! Alright, that's perhaps a little exaggerated, small hamlets, few houses, rarely more than three or four families.

But still: villages! People who welcomed me in the same way I welcome you today. A tavern with food and drink, vendors, with wares for sale! And I quickly learnt that there were other hamlets like this scattered throughout the whole valley – and with these taciturn, but competent blacksmiths, an experienced hunter and his forest hut and an old friend of my uncle.

Well, at least, it's what I thought back then, a friend, but the truth is...

... but that's another story.

2 The Valley

The landscape in which you play is simply called **The Valley**. In the northern part of the map a river flows from East to West, forming the valley. North and south of the river, the terrain ascends, finally turning into mountains with high summits to the south, while rising more gently into a wooden highland to the north.

There are numerous streams, the river flows through 3 to 4 big lakes and there are also 3 smaller closed lakes on the map. All stretches of water are shallow enough to walk through. You can't drown and don't have to swim either. The only difference is that you move much slower in deep water than on land.

The terrain visible on the map is larger than the accessible area in the game which is a square, approximately 2 x 2 km large.

If you leave the playable area, you are teleported roughly 10 m back and Racimir says that he doesn't want to leave the valley, since it is now his home.

When running, traveling 1 km in the game takes approximately 3 minutes in real life. This corresponds more or less to the distance between *Gostovia* and *Denica* or *Rolnica* and *Baranica*.

1 minute in real life corresponds to 30 minutes in the game, meaning a 24 hour day in the game lasts 48 minutes, when playing without a break. When you open the menu (e.g., the map or the inventory), the in-game-time will be paused and all actions will be suspended. When you get attacked, you can choose a weapon of your choice in the inventory, without risking any damage.

There are, in total, 10 villages in the valley and also the hermit Sambor. The villages have different sizes, some of them are just bigger farms, whereas others are surrounded by a palisade and have various vendors.

Furthermore, you find smaller camps, discarded backpacks or broken down handcarts, where you can often find a few objects over and over again. These places spawn randomly at the beginning of each season.

The numerous animals always spawn in specific regions and the places where you find the resources (forests, caves, clay pits, reed etc.) are fixed.

Henceforth, we will take a closer look at all the places where you can find specific resources and at all the events which can happen in the valley.

We begin with a larger map of the valley and of all the villages you can visit:

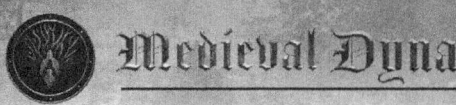

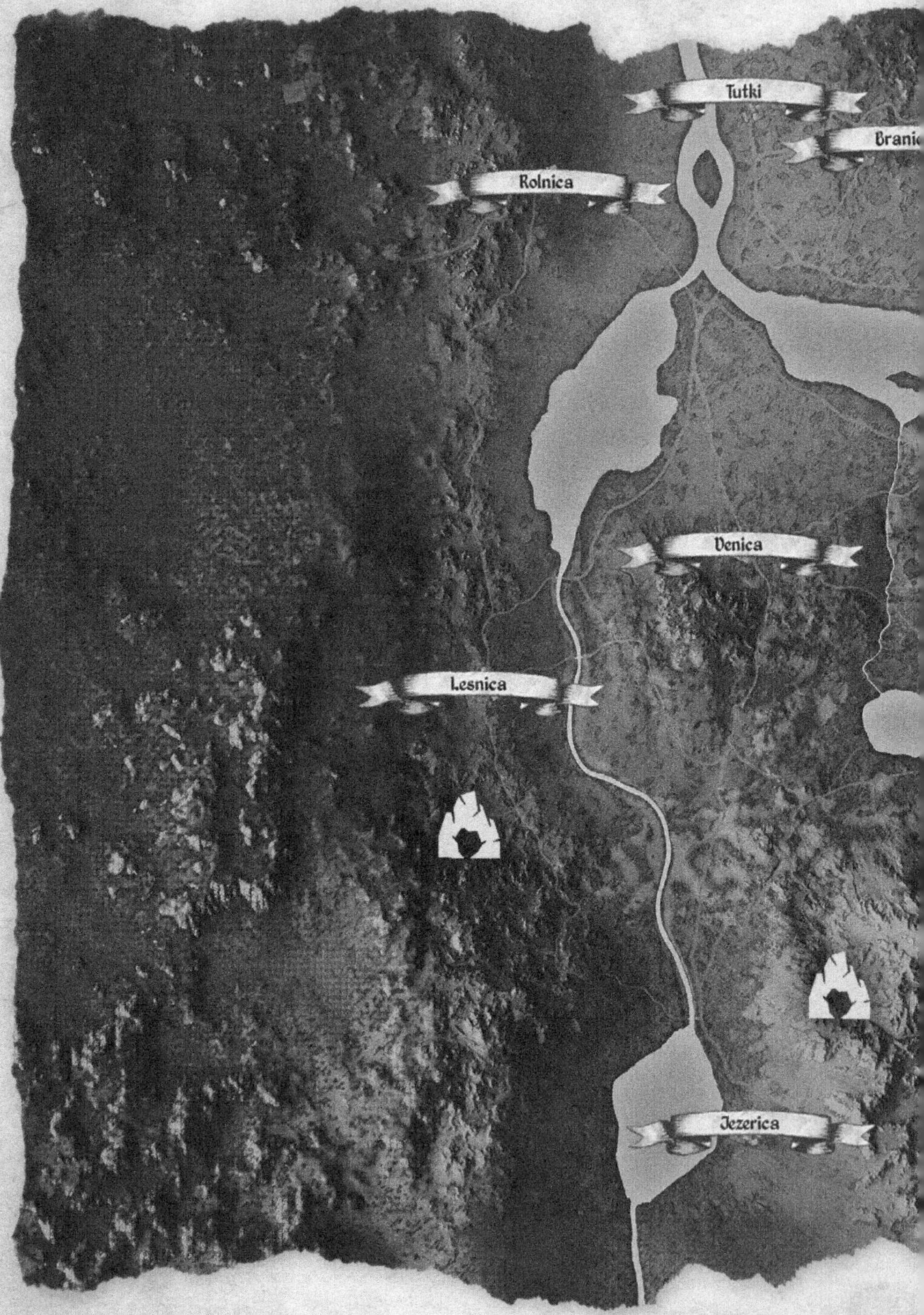

Medieval Dynasty

Tutki

Branie

Rolnica

Venica

Lesnica

Jezerica

ica

Borowo

Gostovia

Hornica

100m

N

2.1 Villages

Gostovia

Description

Gostovia is probably the first village in Medieval Dynasty you will visit. At the same time, it's an important center in the valley as the castellan *Uniegost* lives there. We have to pay him taxes every spring. Furthermore, he has some tasks in store for *Racimir* (the player) which will shed more light on his and *His Uncles Iordan* history.

The second person in Gostovia, who provides you with several quests is the young farmer *Alwin*. You will help him to rise above his farmer's life.

Since the village is relatively big, you can find some objects you can steal. But beware: if someone sees you, you lose prestige (Dynasty Reputation!) – an attempt is enough (e.g., opening a chest, even if it's empty).

You can purchase *Cows* and *Geese* for your village in Gostovia.

Vendors

> Innkeeper Dobroniega: beverages, fruits, meat

> Cook Adelina: food

> Farmer Edwin: seeds, farming tools, fertiliser

> Cow breeder Sobiemir: cows, manure, animal feed, buckets

In proximity

The village of *Borowo* is just opposite of Gostovia and can be reached quickly via two bridges. A lot of reeds grow at the river near Gostovia. There can be an overturned cart near the bridge, east of the road. In the West, on the left side of the road leading out of Gostovia, there can be another one in the forest.

In the western forest, you can also find clay deposits with a forgotten shovel in it – lucky you! (The shovel is a random spawn).

The region near Gostovia offers some good spots to build up your village because almost all resources are near. Besides, you always have to pay taxes in Gostovia and you receive a lot of quests there.

South-east of Gostovia, you can find a picturesque waterfall where you can build a nice village with beautiful surroundings.

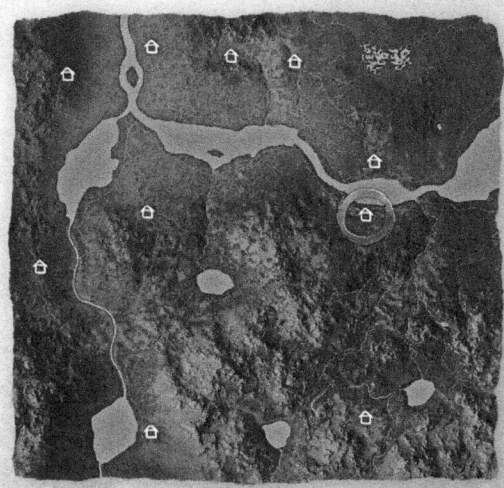

Medieval Dynasty

Borowo

Description

Borowo is situated just opposite of *Gostovia* and is easily accessible via two bridges. The village is a lot smaller and only offers a few interesting things.

You can, however, buy *Chickens* there and keeping a henhouse is normally the first form of animal breeding you do. *Inga* offers everything you need for this.

You will visit vendor *Falibor* during a couple of quests.

If the money of the vendors in Gostovia does not suffice to sell everything you would like to, you can quickly reach Borowo to sell your remaining goods.

Vendors

> Hen breeder Inga: eggs, manure, feathers, animal feed

> Craftsman Falibor: baskets, jugs, cups, plates, torches

In proximity

In the forest north-east of Borowo you come across wisents. Be careful, these European buffaloes are aggressive and dangerous!

If you follow the river east, you reach a big see. There are a lot of reeds there as well as a large flat surface which is ideal to erect a big, beautiful village. Gostovia and Borowo are in immediate vicinity but the other villages are far away.

If you follow the path east of Borowo to the North, you encounter hermit Sambor. On your way, you pass a damaged fence with a broken down cart at the bottom of the slope (random spawn).

Baranica

Description

Baranica is a small village situated on a high ridge. The herbalist Norbert has settled there. He sells cheap potions, in case you can't make them by yourself.

If you want to breed *Sheep*, you have to visit the sheep breeder *Alina* somewhat north of the village. She offers everything you need for this.

Apart from the obligatory campfires with travelers you find in all villages, Baranica does not have much more to offer.

Vendors

> Herbal vendor Norbert: herbs, mushrooms, potions
> Sheep breeder Alina: manure, animal feed, wool, buckets, shearing scissors

In proximity

East of Baranica, you can find a clay deposit.

Furthermore, there is a big flat surface in the East, which would be an ideal spot for a very large village. Since many trees would have to be removed, you require many axes and shovels.

Even further East, there is a swampland (clearly visible on the map) and behind that hermit Sambor in his hermitage.

There is a cave approximately 250 meters north-east of *Branica*. You can find a pickaxe and ore there.

Follow the way north from Baranica and you will reach a fork with a signpost. Every now and then, you can find a broken down cart there. South of Baranica, you find a lot of reed along the see.

At first sight, Baranica doesn't seem like an attractive location for a settlement, but you can find all you need there: wood, clay, reed, metal (in the north-western cave).

East of Baranica there is a wonderful hunting area for wolves, boars, lynxes and moose.

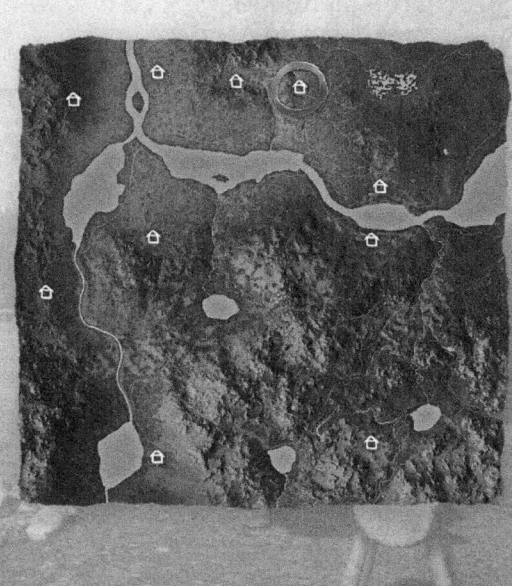

Branica

Description

Branica is a small farm in the highland which is not far away from *Baranica*.

Seamstress Lubomira is in a constant rivalry with the other seamstress of the valley, *Karolina* from *Hornica*. You can try settling this in a quest or get between their fronts. If you choose right, you can get expensive shoes for free. This little quest can also start with the seamstress from *Denica* or the seamstress from your own village!

Bogdan offers planks, in case you can't produce them yet.

You can steal some materials, thread and coins from the chests, but don't get caught!

Vendors

› Lumberjack Bogdan: planks, wood, stone axes
› Seamstress Lubomira: clothes, shoes, pouches, threads

In proximity

You can find a cave directly north-east of Branica within viewing distance. Many other caves are situated on almost impassable terrain, where building is almost impossible. South of the cave you have enough space for a settlement, where you would also have two villages nearby. In fact, this is an interesting place for a mountain settlement.

Follow the road to the west in direction of *Tutki*. East of a small fork, you can find a broken down cart, in which you can only find wool or feathers.

Hunting areas are a bit further away from Branica. You have to proceed to the south to the river meadows (boars, foxes, wisents) or to the west between *Tutki* and *Branica* to hunt deers.

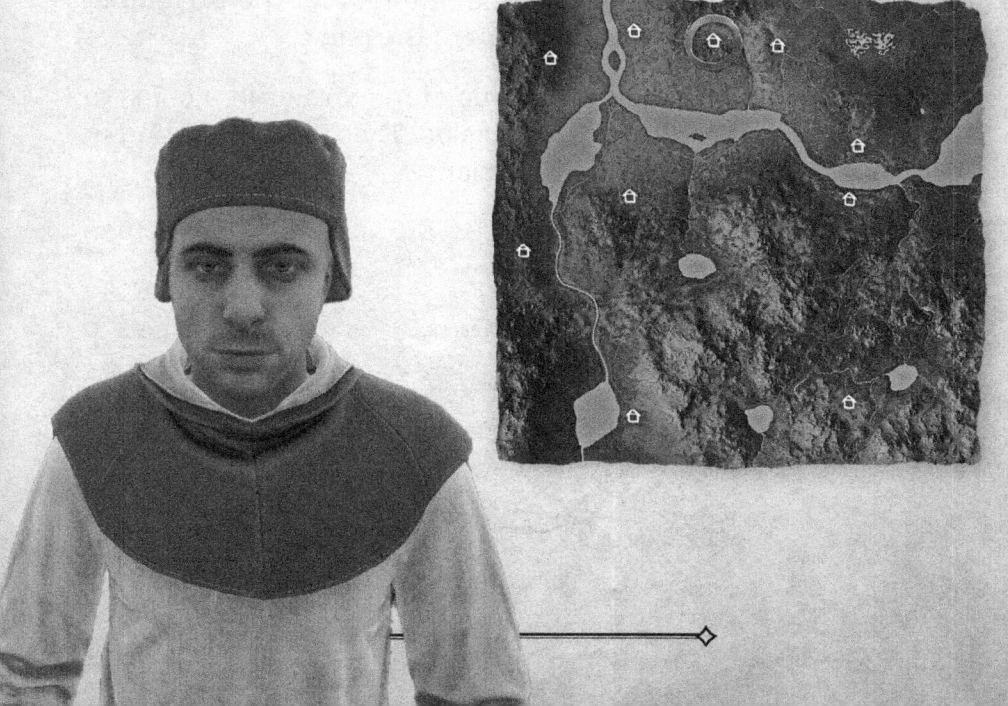

Tutki

Description

Tutki is a small and relatively new village. In an early version of the game, it was the place where Racimir's story began. The farmer *Rajmund* was the first point of interest for the player, but this changed during the development of the game.

In Tutki, you can find a bow and some stone arrows in a chest in the remote hunting lodge near the fields. These make hunting at the beginning of the game much easier.

The *Donkeys* you can buy from *Amanda* can carry more than horses.

Wolrad, who was a member of your *Uncle's Iordan* group, lives in Tutki (See his picture on the right).

Vendors

> Donkey breeder Radochna: saddles, manure, animal feed, horseshoes

> Hunter Rajmund: all bows, stone arrows, knives, spears, waterskins, meat, leather, fur, salt

Rajmund sells you the locations of mammals and birds and marks them on your map.

In proximity

North and north-eastern of Tutki, you can find deers in the dense birch forest. You can track other animals south-east in direction of the river (wisent, boar) or heading east in direction of Branica (wolves, deers).

South-east, there is a small isle which is perfect to build an idyllic farm.

There are reeds at the southern bridge over the river.

The cave near *Branica* is not too far away.

West of the river, halfway to Rolnica or near the river south of Branica, you find clay.

There are moose, lynxes and badgers in the surroundings.

Rolnica

Description

Rolnica is a bigger mountain village very far in the north-east of the map. You'll find a few things to steal in the chests of the houses. There are also things standing around in the village, you could steal.

From the vendors *Nadar* and *Irmina*, you can buy nearly everything you need to farm. Rolnica is the only village where you can buy *pigs*.

Furthermore, you can find *Tomira* in Rolnica, one of the two herbalists of the valley.

As there are three vendors in Rolnica, this village is a good place in the north-west of the map to sell many goods.

A quest from the innkeeper *Dobroniega* from *Gostovia* leads you to Nadar in Rolnica in search of a missing rye delivery. You will find

Nadar's missing messenger injured at the waterfall by the stream east of *Denica*!

Vendors

> Farmer Nadar: seeds, fertiliser, animal feed, fruits, cereals, straw, farming tools

> Herbalist Tomira: herbs, mushrooms, potions

> Pig breeder Irmina: meat, manure, animal feed

In proximity

You'll find clay to the east in direction of the river.

For huntable game, you have to run a bit but there is enough around the village.

Caves are far from Rolnica (east near *Branica* and south near *Lesnica*).

The region in the triangle made by *Tutki*, *Rolnica* and *Denica* offers lovely landscapes alongside the river, near the bridges and enough space to build the settlement of your dreams.

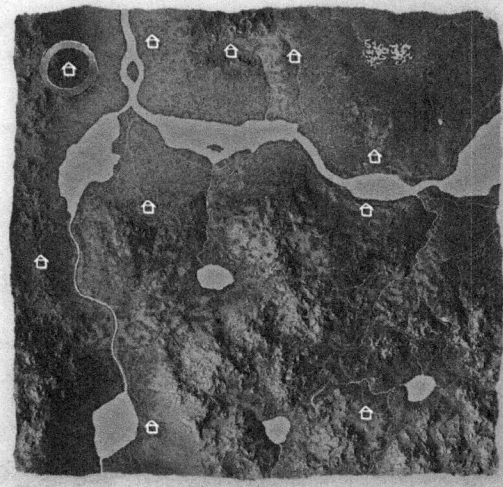

A small drawback: the birch trees, which are mainly found there, only yield 2 trunks per tree.

Denica

Description

Denica is situated between the forest of the river meadows and the mountainous region in the South. This village is relatively big and protected by a palisade.

As there are 3 vendors in Denica, you have enough possibilities to sell a big amount of goods. You can buy *Goats* here, but there is no animal breeder .

There are some objects in the village you can steal, but none of high quality.

As part of Sambor's quest line you'll find *Fenenna*, the precocious „vendor" here.

Vendors

> Farmer Dagobert: seeds, fertilizer, animal feed, fruits, vegetables, cereals, straw, farming tools

> Seamstress Matylda: clothes, shoes, pouches, threads

> Cook Kinga: food

In proximity

You can find enough game in the surrounding woods of Denica. A small hill rises in the south (with enough stone to mine) and behind it, on the right side of the road, there is a clay deposit.

A bit further to the south-east, there is an idyllic lake in the forest. From time to time, you can find abandoned hunting camps around it. West of the lake in direction of the clay deposit, there is a large flat surface which is perfect for a village with fields.

South-west of Denica, on the road to *Lesnica*, an overturned cart can appear at the fork or at the northern bridge of the river a camp with fishing equipment can spawn.

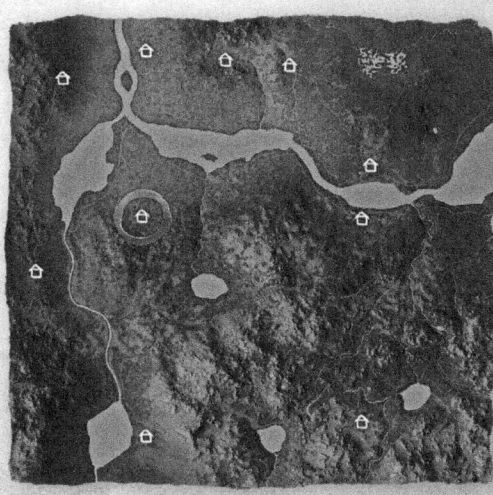

Lesnica

Description

Lesnica is a mining village surrounded by a small fence on a hill in the west of the valley.

Four vendors in one village are a lot. However, there is neither one who sells cooked food, nor one who sells animals. If you need some cooked food, you have to continue to Denica or Jezerica or cook by yourself over a fire.

In Lesnica, there is also one of the two blacksmiths of the valley. You can buy tools, weapons, arrows and bolts made of all metals from *Teobald*.

One of Alwin's quests will lead you to Lesnica to the hunter Gizela.

Vendors

> Hunter Gizela: all bows, stone arrows, knives, spears, water-skins, meat, leather, fur, salt

Gizela sells you the locations of mammals and birds and marks them on your map.

> Lumberjack: planks, wood, stone axes

> Blacksmith Teobald: tools and weapons made of metal, ores

> Miner: stones, ores, clay, salt, mining tools

In proximity

North of Lesnica, in the hilly area, there are 2 clay deposits.

Follow the path south of the village through the forest until you get to crossroads. Then continue to the west and to the cave. Be careful, there are often one or two bears around!

If you want to build near Lesnica, prepare yourself for a lot of lumberjack work!

Jezerica

Description

Jezerica is a small fishing village at a mountain lake in the south-west mountains surrounding the valley.

In Uniegost's story, a quest will lead you to Domagoj in Jezerica. A small tip: It's best to take a crossbow with you.

Apart from this, there are few reasons to visit this village. There are no worth while tools or animals to buy here. However, if you want to build and live remotely in the middle of nowhere, you've come to the right place.

Vendors

> Fisher Bytomir: fish, salt, fishing spears

Gizela sells you the locations of mammals and birds and marks them on your map.

> Innkeeper Nieluba: beverages and some food

In proximity

Follow the road to the north of the village, pass by a small bridge until you reach a fork. Between the 2 roads, you will find a clay deposit where the right hand roads turns to the east.

North-east, on the other side of the mountain, there is a cave. You can follow the path from Jezerica but hereby you will make a long detour. It's faster to go directly over the mountain slope. Be careful: 1-2 bears wander around north the cave.

Reed grows south of the fishing hut at the river.

If you follow the river to the north, you will get to a big and flat area, which offers a perfect place to build. It lies in the middle of *Jezerica* and *Lesnica*. Therefore, you don't have to walk too far to reach the blacksmith and the other vendors of Lesnica. The cave in the west is also really near. You're just next to a clay deposit and the second cave in the East can also be reached easily. There is enough space available for fields. The disadvantage is the long way to *Gostovia* for paying taxes every year. But as soon as you get married, you can send your wife in your place.

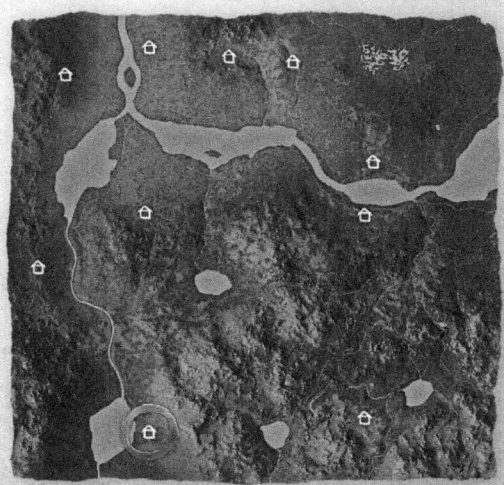

Hornica

Description

Hornica is the biggest village of the valley. It is a mining and trading settlement on the southern edge of the map. With 6 vendors it has the most of all the villages. Some quests will lead you to Hornica again and again.

Vendors

> Blacksmith Jan: weapons and tools of metal, ores, arrows

> Seamstress Karolina: clothes, pouches, bags, backpacks

> Horse breeder Leonard: saddles, animal feed, horseshoes

> Miner: ores, salt, stones, mining tools

> Cook: food and ingredients

> Innkeeper Helga: beverages and a bit of food

In proximity

Not only the village has a lot to offer, you will find various kinds of animals in the forest surrounding the village.

The lakes on the west and east offer a good settlement and hunting area.

At the eastern lake, bears live in the southeast and if you follow the stream further you will arrive at a cave.

Another cave is situated in the mountains north-west of Hornica. Follow the path to the north until you get to the second fork just after a small bridge over a stream and keep west. Be careful, bears wander around that cave too.

The lake west of Hornica offers nice building sites. Reeds and the cave by *Jezerica* are nearby.

However, the lake east offers more building areas and it is possible to build next to the cave there. In the forest north of the lake, you can find more animals than at the lake west of Hornica.

To the east, clay can be found in the forest north of the lake. Follow the stream flowing to the north. A little hidden, on its left side, in the forest, you can find a clay deposit.

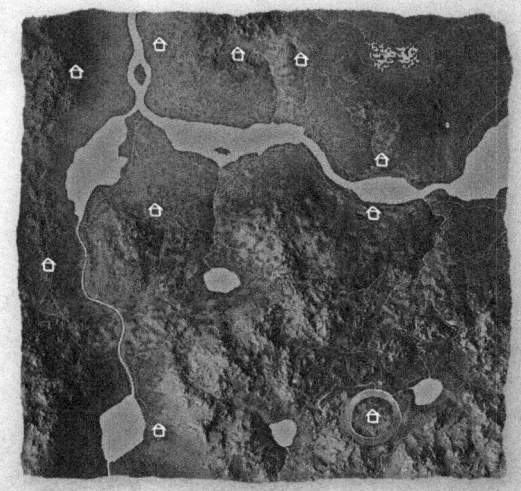

Sambor the Hermit

Description

Sambor the hermit lives secluded in the north-eastern area of the map. A quest from *Uniegost* will lead you to him. Be warned: Sambor is a harsh fellow but also a chatterbox!

Collect the wooden deer figures near his house, go back and talk to Sambor, to get another quest!

Vendors

> none

In proximity

Sambor didn't establish himself here for no reason. You can find various kinds of animals as ,e.g., deers and wisents in the expansive forests to the west and south.

Numerous clay deposits can be found there.

Immediately north of Sambor's house, you can find the first deposit and the second one is slightly east of the house. You can find the third one north of the swamp.

The next cave is near *Branica*, which is quite far away.

There is straw at the lake south of Sambor's house. This is also further away. The swamp in the west is closer, there you can also find some straw.

The area surrounding Sambor's hut is very woody. If you want to build your village in the surroundings, you should take a "Robin Hood Style" into consideration or get ready for a lot of lumberjack work.

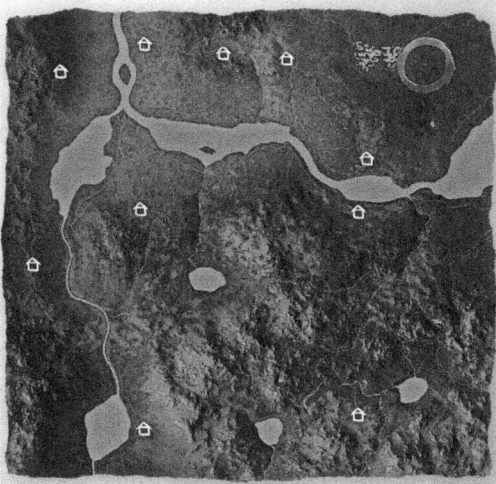

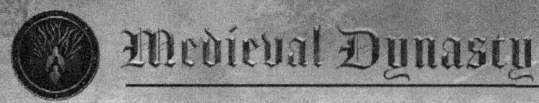
2.2 Waggoners

Near each village you will find a man with a cart. These waggoners offer you the possibility to be driven to another town for money. However, especially at the beginning of the game, not everyone can afford it; the prices are quite high.

From Gostovia to Borovo it costs only 80 coins, which you can easily afford but is pointless because walking is almost as fast. From Rolnica to Hornica, one of the longest routes, the waggoner charges 660 coins. It is better to invest this money in tools and weapons in the beginning.

If you don't want to travel across the whole valley but want to reach closer places quickly, you usually have to pay a price between 300 and 500 coins. These quick trips are intentionally expensive, because you should get to know the world around you; find animals, mushrooms, herbs and special places in the beginning. Later in the game, when you have money flowing, it won't be a big deal to spend that much money.

Medieval Dynasty

2.3 Points of Interest

Apart from villages, you also come upon smaller points of interest, where you can find objects, resources or valuables. Especially iron weapons and iron tools are very useful at the beginning.

These points are:

» Crashed and broken down handcarts

» Hunting camps with a campfire and sleeping bags

» Lost tools from workers (e.g., an iron shovel stuck in a clay deposit or a forgotten iron pickaxe in front of a cave)

Most of them spawn randomly. The places they can show up at are fixed but whether they actually do is determined by chance at the beginning of each new season. The map on the right shows you some of these places, but others are just waiting for you to find them! Since version 1.0, over 100 new locations have been added in numerous updates!

Look particularly near broken fences, caves, clay deposits, road forks, crossroads, or conspicuous places – most of the time you'll find something.

Overturned Carts and Buried Treasures

You can find overturned carts near roads or at forks.

You recognize buried treasures by a cairn and a shovel stuck in the soil next to it. Remove all the stones because you often find bags with money or other things under them.

Items on the Ground

You can find forgotten items
practically everywhere,
whether an axe in the forest,
a pickaxe in the rock face or
barrels full of materials in
front of or inside caves.

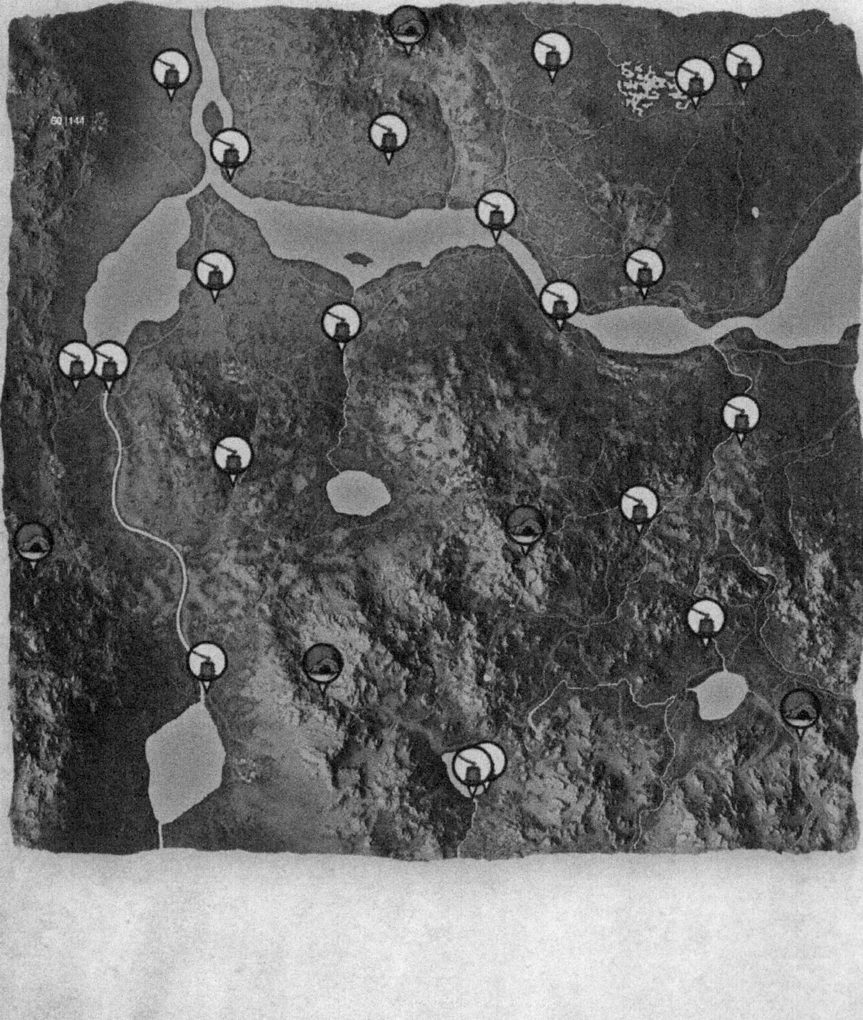

Abandoned Camps

Hunters or lumberjacks have set up these camps and left some things there. Take what you need and can carry!

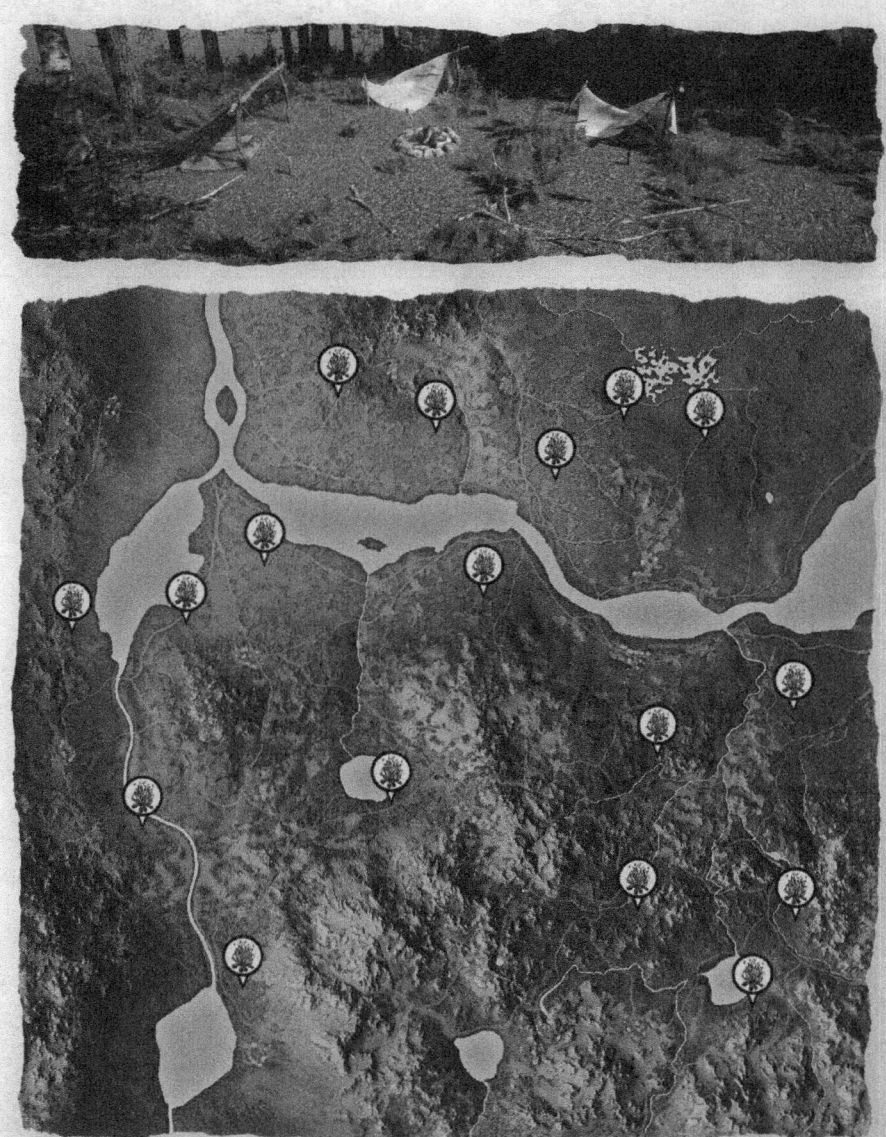

Medieval Dynasty

2.4 Resources

To build and craft objects, you need raw materials. You can find these resources everywhere in the valley. You can buy every raw material and every manufactured object from the various vendors of the valley.

Here we show you where you can find all the basics resources. We don't list manufactured resources here (e.g., firewood can be made of logs for further use).

Icon	Raw material/ resource	Collect with	Remark
	Log	Axe: cut down trees Shovel: tree stump Woodshed	Birch tree:2 Spruce tree: 3 Maple tree: 4
	Sticks	Collect from the floor Cut down trees Woodshed Break off branches	Birch tree: a lot Spruce tree: normal Maple tree: a few
	Stones	Collect from the floor Pickaxe: mine rocks Mine or excavation shed	
	Feathers	Cut down trees Bird traps, hunt birds Chicken or goose houses Nest and hunting lodge	
	Straw	Collect reed Transform crops into grains in the barn Excavation cave	
	Limestone	Pickaxe: mine rocks Mine or excavation shed	
	Clay	Shovel: dig up clay Excavation shed	

Icon	Raw material/ resource	Collect with	Remark
	Leather	Hunt animals Hunting lodge	
	Fur	Hunt animals Hunting lodge	
	Wool	Sheep in the Fold	
	Salt	Pickaxe: caves Mine	
	Copper Ore	Pickaxe: caves Mine	
	Tin Ore	Pickaxe: caves Mine	
	Iron Ore	Pickaxe: caves Mine	
	Seeds (All)	From the corresponding field	The first seed has to be bought
	Honeycomb	Apiary	

Respawn of Resources

Raw materials you have depleted will respawn, meaning they are available again after some time.

» Almost all mineable and collectible resources respawn with the change of seasons: mined stones, ores and salt in caves and mines, hunted animals and fish, and clay deposits. Reeds and twigs have a season break before respawning. Sticks and stones on the ground take 1 year.

» Berries, herbs and mushrooms depend on the season. You can only find and collect them during specifics seasons. Even cultivated plants like wheat and cabbages depend on the seasons. You'll learn more about this in the chapters about herbalism and farming.

» Felled trees respawn after 2 years, provided the stump is still there. If you dig out the stump, no tree will regenerate.

Caves and Mines

There are only 5 caves in the valley. You can see their position on the map on page 94 of the book.

You can often find bears around the caves and tools at their entrance (e.g., pickaxes).

In the caves, you can extract salt, copper and tin ores. By doing this, you automatically get stones. Copper and tin can be manufactured into bars at the smithy or you can make bronze bars out of them. You can use the bars afterwards to craft tools and weapons.

Caves are very dark and even a torch doesn't light up the passages completely.

As soon as you have 5000 experience in the *Building Technology*, you can build a mine. The "Mine building" just has to be placed at the entrance of the cave and the cave transforms into a mine with the following benefits:

> - You can assign a worker to the mine.
> - You can find iron in the mine.
> - The mine is lighted and wooden signs show you the exit.

Metal tools are expensive and can also be sold for a good price. That's why possessing a mine and a smithy is really worthwhile.

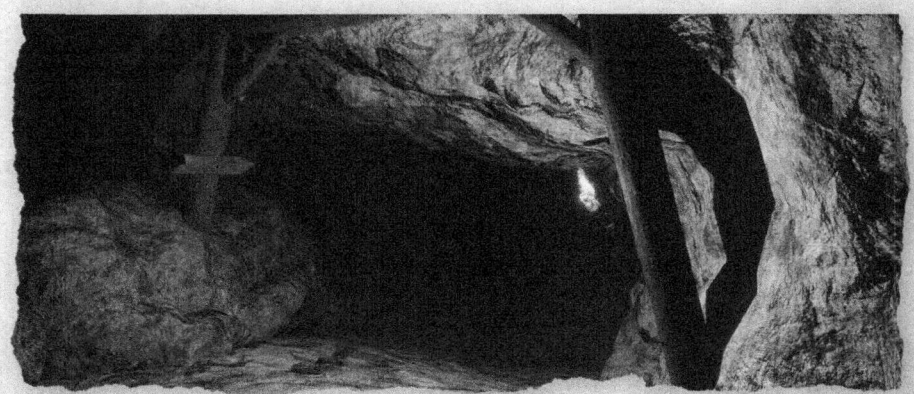

Clay Deposits

You need clay in your workshop for pottery, in order to make receptacles and bottles, which you need in the tavern, for potions and decorations.

Furthermore, you can make daub out of clay and straw in the barn, which you can use to plaster your houses. Plastered houses need less firewood, because their insulation is better. The mood of inhabitants of insulated houses is better.

You can find clay at these places:

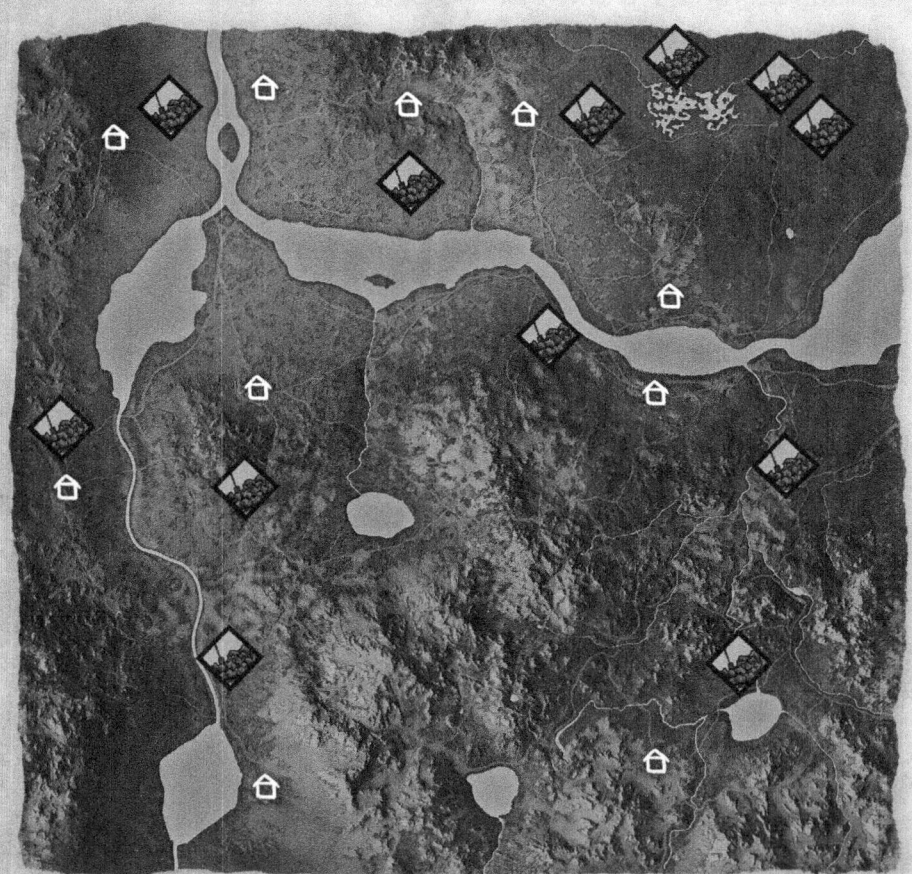

Medieval Dynasty

Reed

At the beginning of the game reed is your only source of straw to cover the roofs of the houses or to make daub. Reed can be found near almost every lake, river or in the swamp in the North-East:

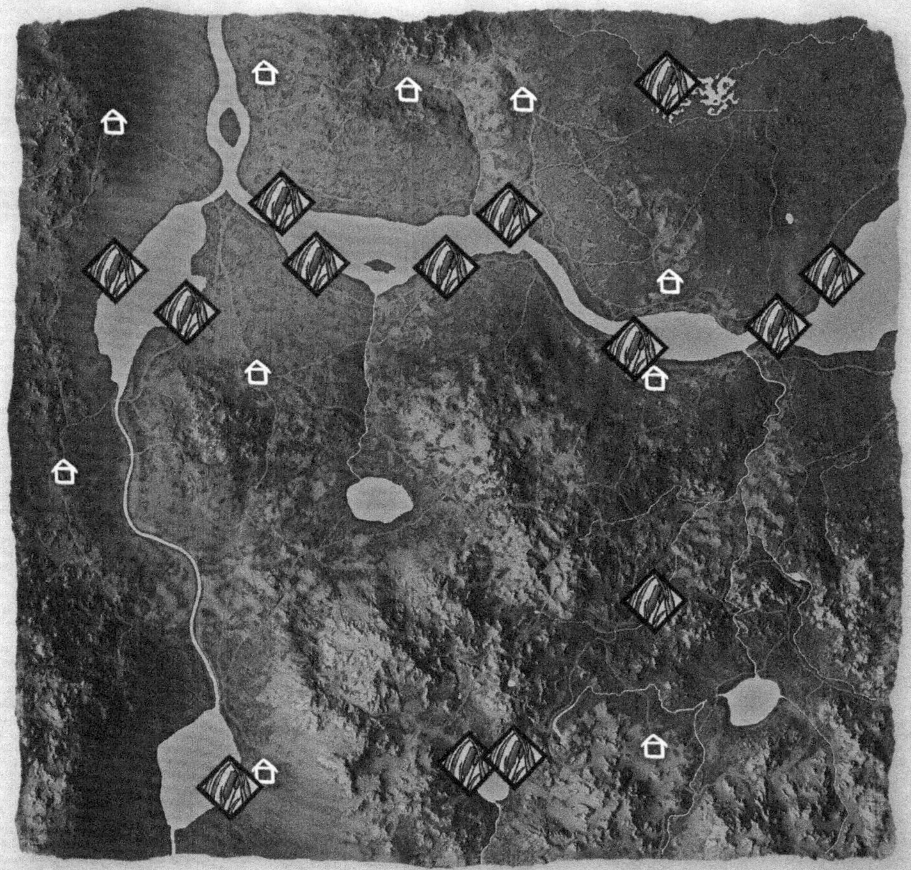

2.5   Vendors

You can find various vendors in every village. Some have a strictly limited offer, whereas other have a wide range of products.

Until you are able to craft many things by yourself, you possibly need to buy some objects. You will ,e.g., need to buy your first seeds for your fields and also your first animals to begin with animal husbandry.

You can't craft iron tools at the beginning but they last longer and speed up work (e.g., an iron axe only needs 3 hits to fell a tree, the stone axe needs 5).

Vendors in General

Each vendor type offers the same products at the same prices. It doesn't make any difference if you go to the blacksmith of Lesnica, Hornica or the village you buy your clothes in.

The list of products is always the same, but to some degree their amount varies.

The amount of money they have also varies. Most vendors have between 1000 and 2500 coins. A vendor cannot buy more than he can afford.

The purchasing price of an item is always 50% higher than the price that is indicated to you in its description. However, when you sell an item you only receive half of its value. For example: a honeycomb has a value of 10 coins. You can sell it for 5 coins or buy it for 15 coins from a vendor.

The prices each vendor offers are identical. You can lower the prices by 10%, 20% and 30% by unlocking and increasing the ability *Barter* in the *Diplomacy* skill tree.

You can sell every item to every vendor. Thus, you don't have to find a seamstress to sell your shoes, the innkeeper and the lumberjack will buy them just as well.

If you sell items to a vendor he does not usually offer, he will keep them in his inventory until you buy them back (at the full price) or until the next season begins.

The amount of money and the inventory of each vendor is reset at the beginning of a new season.

List of vendors

In the village descriptions of this book, you can look up which vendors you find in each village.

In the list below, you find all the vendors of the valley and their location. Many vendors always have the same name, others have a different name from game to game. When it comes to breeding animals, you don't buy them from the vendor directly but by selecting the animal you want. The corresponding vendor only sells breeding accessories and associated products (like animal feed, manure and saddles). The given prices are the default values. The merchant sells the goods 50% more expensive and buys them for 50% less (example: value 80; you buy for 120; you sell for 40). The prices can be affected by skills.

General vendors:

Innkeeper:	Gostovia, Jezerica, Hornica
Cook:	Gostovia, Denica, Hornica
Lumberjack:	Branica, Lesnica
Miner:	Hornica, Lesnica
Herbalist:	Baranica, Rolnica
Blacksmith:	Lesnica, Hornica
Seamstress:	Branica, Denica, Hornica
Craftsman:	Borowo
Farmer:	Rolnica, Gostovia, Denica
Hunter:	Lesnica, Sambor
Fisher:	Jezerica

Breeders:

Sheep breeder:	Baranica
Pig breeder:	Rolnica
Horse breeder:	Hornica
Donkey breeder:	Tutki
Chicken breeder:	Borowo, Rolnica
Cow breeder:	Gostovia
Only sells geese:	Gostovia
Only sells goats:	Denica

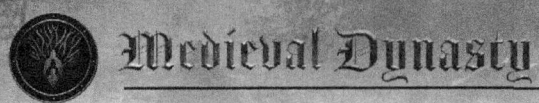
Innkeepers:

Dobroniega in Gostovia | Nieluba in Jezerica | Helga in Hornica

Item	Weight	Value	Item	Weight	Value
Apple	0.09	3	Cherry Juice	0.6	120
Apple Juice	0.60	130	Cherry Wine	0.6	240
Apple Wine	0.60	250	Cabbage	0.2	3
Berry	0.05	0,2	Mead	0.4	280
Berry Juice	0.60	110	Plum	0.07	2
Berry Wine	0.60	190	Plum Juice	0.6	150
Honeycomb	0.10	10	Plum Wine	0.6	270
Pear	0.10	3	Rye Beer	0.5	240
Pear Juice	0.6	140	Beetroot	0.15	3
Pear Wine	0.6	260	Salted Meat	0.25	16
Egg	0.05	10	Dried Meat	0.2	8
Fish Meat	0.2	4	Wheat Beer	0.5	260
Meat	0.2	3	Onion	0.1	2
Oat Ale	0.5	180	Beer Bottle	0.35	50

Item	Weight	Value	Item	Weight	Value
Oat Beer	0.5	230	Hop	0.02	3
Carrot	0.1	2	Mead Bottle	0.3	50
Cherry	0.05	2	Wine Bottle	0.5	60
Bucket of water	2	30	Waterskin with Water	0,25	170

Cooks:

Adelina in Gostovia | Kinga in Denica | Hornica

Item	Weight	Value	Item	Weight	Value
Apple	0.09	3	Flatbread	0.05	80
Porridge with Apple	0.25	60	Flatbread with Onions	0.1	100
Berry	0.05	0,2	Meat	0.2	3
Porridge with Berries	0.25	50	Meat with Gravy	0.55	40
Honeycomb	0.1	10	Meat Pie	0.1	220
Pear	0.1	3	Meat Tart	0.1	180
Pear Tart	0.1	190	Roasted Fish Meat	0.2	6
Porridge	0.2	30	Roasted Meat	0.2	5
Egg	0.05	10	Vegetable Soup	0.8	100
Stew	0.75	40	Salted Fish Meat	0.2	18
Fish Meat	0.2	4	Dried Fish Meat	0.2	10
Fisch Tart	0.1	180	Oat Roll	0.1	110
Gruel	0.2	30	Beetroot	0.15	3
Carrot	0.1	2	Scrambled Eggs	0.2	60
Cherry	0.05	2	Scrambled Eggs with Mushroom	0.2	70
Cherry Pie	0.1	240	Salted Meat	0.25	16
Cabbage	0.2	3	Soup	0.75	50

Item	Weight	Value
Potage	0.7	50
Multigrain Bread	0.15	170
Poppy Seed Pie	0.1	230
Fruit Pie	0.1	210
Fruit Tart	0.1	190
Plum	0.07	2
Plum Tart	0.1	200
Mushroom Soup	0.2	30
Rye bread	0,15	140
Cheese	0,2	100
Bucket of Water	2	30

Item	Weight	Value
Dried Meat	0.2	8
Wheat Bread	0.15	150
Wheat Roll	0.1	130
White Bread	0.15	120
Onion	0.1	2
Hop	0.02	3
Flour	0.01	5
Poppy	0.05	3
Potage	0,7	50
Quark	02	50
Waterskin with Water	0,25	140

Medieval Dynasty

Blacksmiths:

Teobald in Lesnica | Jan in Hornica

Item	Weight	Value	Item	Weight	Value
Bow	1.25	90	Stone Knife	0.5	40
Bronze Knife	0.75	220	Stone Spear	2.5	100
Bronze Spear	2	330	Fishing Spear	2.5	100
Iron Cross-bow	1.25	730	Bronze Axe	3.5	350
Iron Spear	2	410	Bronze Hoe	2	220
Iron Knife	0.75	300	Bronze Hammer	2	220
Wooden Crossbow	1	150	Bronzes Shovel	3	360
Wooden Spear	1.5	20	Bronze Shearing Scissors	1	110
Copper Knife	0.5	110	Bronze Scythe	4	360
Copper Spear	2	170	Bronze Sickle	1.5	290
Longbow	1.25	230	Bronze Pick-axe	5	360
Recurve Bow	1.25	320	Bucket	2	30
Iron Shear-ing Scissors	1	140	Stone Sickle	0.75	45
Iron Scythe	4	500	Bronze Bolt	0.01	11
Iron Pickaxe	5	500	Bronze Ar-row	0.01	11
Iron Hoe	2	300	Iron Bolt	0.01	13

Item	Weight	Value
Iron Hammer	2	300
Iron Sickle	1.5	400
Iron Axe	3.5	490
Iron Shovel	3	500
Wooden Hoe	2	30
Wooden Shovel	2	25
Wooden Hammer	1	30
Copper Axe	3	180
Copper Hoe	2	110
Copper Hammer	2	110
Copper Shovel	3	180
Copper Sickle	1	140
Stone Axe	2.5	40
Stone Hoe	2.5	45
Toy Sword	0,75	45

Item	Weight	Value
Iron Arrow	0.01	13
Wooden Bolt	0.01	7
Copper Bolt	0.01	9
Copper Arrow	0.01	9
Stone Arrow	0.01	7
Iron Horse-shoes	4	250
Bronze Bar	1	60
Iron Bar	1	90
Iron Ore	1	40
Copper Bar	1	30
Copper Ore	1	12
Tin Bar	1	25
Tin Ore	1	10
Iron Spiked Cudgel	2	180
Throwing Stone	0,2	0,2

Medieval Dynasty

Seamstresses:

Lubomira in Branica | Karolina in Hornica | Matylda in Denica

Item	Weight	Value	Item	Weight	Value
Bag	0.5	180	Simple Small Backpack	0.5	190
Simple Bag	0.15	50	Simple Linen Shirt	0.25	200
Waterskin	0.25	170	Fur Boots	0.35	250
Pouch	0.5	180	Felt Hat	0.15	520
Thick Leather Gloves	0.15	180	Felt Vest	0.7	590
Noble Shoes	0.1	340	Flat Straw Hat	0.15	130
Noble Boots	0.2	420	Quilted Vest	0.8	740
Simple Shoes	0.15	100	Large Saddlebag	4	610
Simple Tunic	0.5	380	Large Pouch	1	260
Simple Backpack	1	260	Coif	0.05	150
Simple Large Backpack	1.5	380	Trousers	0.3	200
Trousers with Cuffs	0.35	220	Saddlebag	3	370
Hat	0.1	320	Fancy Shoes	0.15	290
Hat with Lappels	0.1	380	Shoes	0.15	140

   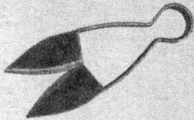

Item	Weight	Value	Item	Weight	Value
Cap	0.05	230	Saddle	2	480
Hood	0.3	330	Boots	0.25	280
Small Saddlebag	2	280	Strawhat	0.2	120
Small Pouch	0.25	110	Baghat	0.2	600
Hose	0.4	370	Tunic	0.5	470
Short Sleeve Tunika	0.45	320	Joined Hose	0.5	460
Long Hood	0.4	480	Flax	0.05	10
Long Fur Hood	0.4	520	Flax Stalk	0.04	5
Linen Shirt	0.25	270	Linen Thread	0.1	50
Cap with Coif	0.1	290	Linen Fabric	0.1	60
Fur Shoes	0.25	170	Wool	0.1	12
Fur Hood	0.35	370	Wool Thread	0.5	100
Fur Capelet	0.25	240	Wool Fabric	0.5	120
Rag Doll	0,15	60			

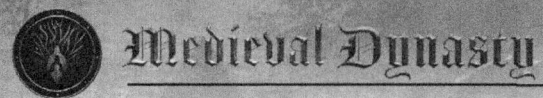
Medieval Dynasty

Lumberjacks:

Bogdan in Branica | Lesnica

Item	Weight	Value
🔨 Stone Axe	2.5	40
🪵 Firewood	0.6	2
Plank	1	4

Item	Weight	Value
Log	2.5	2
Stick	0.1	0.2

Miners:

Lesnica | Hornica

Item	Weight	Value	Item	Weight	Value
Wooden Shovel	2	25	Copper Bar	1	30
Stone Pick-axe	3	45	Copper Ore	1	12
Simple torch	0.5	10	Salt	0.5	8
Torch	0.5	40	Stone	1	0,2
Bronze Bar	1	60	Clay	0.5	0,2
Iron Ore	1	40	Tin Bar	1	25
Limestone	1	12	Tin Ore	1	10

Farmers:

Nadar in Rolnica | Edwin in Gostovia | Dagobert in Denica

Item	Weight	Value	Item	Weight	Value
Bag	0.5	180	Onion	0.1	2
Simple Bag	0.15	50	Apple Tree Seedling	1	180
Wooden Hoe	2	30	Cherry Tree Seedling	1	150
Stone Hoe	2.5	45	Manure	0.25	2
Stone Sickle	0.75	45	Fertilizer	0.5	5
Flat Straw Hat	0.15	130	Flax	0.05	10
Straw hat	0.2	120	Flax Stalk	0.04	5
Apple	0.09	3	Oat	0.05	5
Pear	0.1	3	Oat Grain	0.01	5
Carrot	0.1	2	Hop	0.02	3
Cherry	0.05	2	Hop Plant Seedling	1	250
Cabbage	0.2	3	Carrot Seed	0.01	5
Plum	0.07	2	Cabbage Seed	0.01	8
Beetroot	0.15	3	Daub	0.5	1

Item	Weight	Value		Item	Weight	Value
Flax Seed	0.01	10		Rye Grain	0.01	5
Flour	0.01	5		Beetroot Seed	0.01	8
Poppy	0.05	3		Straw	0.04	0,2
Poppy Seed	0.01	3		Animal Feed	0.2	20
Pear Tree Seedling	1	200		Wheat	0.06	10
Plum Tree Seedling	1	160		Wheat Grain	0.02	10
Rye	0.05	5		Onion Seed	0.01	5

Fishermen:
Bytomir in Jezerica

Item	Weight	Value		Item	Weight	Value
Fishing Spear	2.5	100		Dried Fish Meat	0.2	10
Perch	0.4	15		Pike	0.7	25
Fish Meat	0.2	4		Roach	0.2	2
Salted Fish Meat	0.2	18		Salt	0.5	8

Sheep Breeder:
Alina in Baranica

Item	Weight	Value		Item	Weight	Value
Bronze Shearing Scissors	1	110		Manure	0.25	2
Bucket of Water 10/10	2	180		Animal Feed	0.2	20
Bucket of Milk 10/10	2	180		Wool	0.1	12

Horse Breeder:
Leonard in Hornica

	Item	Weight	Value
	Iron Horse-shoes	4	250
	Large Saddlebag	4	610
	Small Saddlebag	2	280
	Saddle	2	480

	Item	Weight	Value
	Saddlebag	3	370
	Manure	0.25	2
	Animal Feed	0.2	20

Pig Breeder:
Irmina in Rolnica

	Item	Weight	Value
	Meat	0.2	3
	Manure	0.25	2

	Item	Weight	Value
	Animal Feed	0.2	20

Chicken Breeder:
Inga in Borowo

	Item	Weight	Value		Item	Weight	Value
	Egg	0.05	10		Feather	0.01	3
	Manure	0.25	2		Animal Feed	0.2	20

Donkey Breeder:
Radochna in Tutki

	Item	Weight	Value		Item	Weight	Value
	Iron Horse-shoes	4	250		Saddlebag	3	370
	Large Saddlebag	4	610		Manure	0.25	2
	Small Saddlebag	2	280		Animal Feed	0.2	20
	Saddle	2	480				

Cow Breeder:
Sobiemir in Gostovia

Item	Weight	Value	Item	Weight	Value
Bucket of Water 10/10	2	180	Manure	0.25	2
Bucket of Milk 10/10	2	180	Animal Feed	0.2	20

Medieval Dynasty

Craftsman:
Falibor in Borowo

Item	Weight	Value	Item	Weight	Value
Simple Torch	0.5	10	Wooden Wheel	4	40
Torch	0.5	40	Small Wicker Basket	0.5	15
Beer Bottle	0.35	50	Medium Wicker Basket	0.8	20
Wooden Bowl	0.2	4	Clay Cup	0.2	20
Wooden Plate	0.2	4	Clay Mug	0.25	30
Mead Bottle	0.3	50	Clay Bottle	0.5	40
Wine Bottle	0.5	60	Clay Jug	0.5	40
Clay Vial	0.2	20	Clay Bowl	0.4	30
Large Wicker Basket	1.2	25	Wicker Crate	1.6	30
Wooden Cup	0.2	4	Wooden Vial	0.2	3
Wooden Ladle	0.07	3	Wooden Spoon	0.07	3

Hunters:

Gizela in Lesnica | Rajmund in Tutki

Item	Weight	Value
Bow	1.25	90
Wooden Spear	1.5	20
Longbow	1.25	230
Recurve Bow	1.25	320
Stone Knife	0.5	40
Stone Spear	2.5	100
Waterskin	0.25	170

Item	Weight	Value
Meat	0.2	3
Salted Meat	0.25	16
Dried Meat	0.2	8
Feather	0.01	3
Leather	0.25	8
Fur	0.25	6
Salt	0.5	8

Item	Weight	Value		Item	Weight	Value
Stone Arrow	0.01	7				

Herbalists:

Norbert in Baranica | Tomira in Rolnica

Item	Weight	Price		Item	Weight	Price
Potion of Sobriety	0.2	50		St. John's Wort	0.01	0,3
Berry	0.05	0,2		Poison	0.2	40
Bitter Bolete Mushroom	0.1	2		Potion of Friendliness	0.2	80
Broadleaf Plantain	0.01	0,5		Potion of Healing I	0.2	40
Chicory	0.01	0,4		Potion of Healing II	0.2	50
Cure Potion	0.2	50		Potion of Health	0.2	60
Daisy	0.01	0,5		Potion of Instant Healing I	0.2	40
Dandelion	0.01	0,6		Potion of Instant Healing II	0.2	50
Deadly Nightshade	0.01	0,6		Potion of Night Vision	0.2	50
Red Pine Mushroom	0.1	3		Potion of Stamina	0.2	40
Flay Agaric Mushroom	0.1	2		Potion of Strength	0.2	40
Potion of Satiety	0.2	50		Potion of Temperature	0.2	50

Item	Weight	Price	Item	Weight	Price
Henbane	0.01	0,5	Potion of Weight	0.2	60
Potion of Instant Cure	0.2	40	Parasol Mushroom	0.1	3
Bolete Mushroom	0.1	3	Poisoned Iron Bolt	0,01	16
Morel Mushroom	0.1	2	Poisoned Iron Arrow	0,01	16
Thistle	0.01	0,4	Poisoned Wooden Bolt	0,01	10
Potion of Saturation	0.2	40	Poisoned Copper Bolt	0,01	12
Wooly Milkcap Mushroom	0.1	2	Poisoned Copper Arrow	0,01	12
Poisoned Bronze Bolt	0,01	14	Poisoned Stone Arrow	0,01	10
Poisoned Bronze Arrow	0,01	14			

2.6 Quests & Events

You receive quests from inhabitants and many are also automatically assigned. These are subdivided into different categories, which we expand on below.

Chapters

The chapter tasks lead you through the game and make you use its new mechanisms. As soon as you complete a chapter, the next chapter begins immediately.

Chapter tasks do not have to be completed within one season.

You should complete the chapters soon, as this is the fastest way to progress. After completing a chapter, you can build more buildings and the higher your reputation is, the more residents you can recruit. A chapter task cannot fail.

Taxes

You automatically receive the task of *Paying Taxes* at the beginning of spring. You can find them under challenges. Pay your taxes to *Uniegost* in *Gostovia*. If you're married, you can also ask your wife to pay them in your place, but don't forget to give her a present from time to time, or else you will be single again soon.

The amount of taxes depends on the number and type of your buildings and inhabitants. The bigger and better the building, the more taxes it costs. The taxes for a single building also increase steadily with the expansion of your village. There is also a small but not negligible field tax.

In the *Management Screen* under *Houses* you see how much you have to pay for each house. Unfortunately, you only find out the price of a building after having built it. In this book you can find the maximum tax rate of each house in chapter 7.

If you do not pay your taxes during spring, you will incur debts and lose Dynasty reputation. You can always pay your debts to *Uniegost*, but unfortunately the reputation is lost. The correlation here is crucial: the longer you don't pay, the more reputation is gradually lost. It is the loss of reputation that will ultimately lead to your expulsion. So, don't let it get that far.

Story Quests

Story quests tell the story of a few inhabitants. First, there is the story of *Uniegost*, the administrator (castellan) of the village. As his quest line progresses, you'll meet more people who also knew your Uncle Iordan and give you more quests to learn your uncle's whole story.

The second storyline is about the young farmer *Alwin*, who didn't have a lot of change and excitement in his life. You meet Alwin in *Gostovia* too. Most of the time you find him in his fields on the slope, south of the village. You often have to wait for the next season for the next task, so his quest also lasts over a longer period of time. Help him and he rewards you with certain items, which will be very helpful at the beginning! So don't wait to long before beginning his quest, because his reward will not be that interesting in an advanced stage of the game. Story quests expire, although this often takes years - check the times in the *Journal*!

Medieval Dynasty

Side Quests

In addition to the chapters and the story quests, you will get a lot of side quests from inhabitants of the valley. You recognize them on the map by a yellow exclamation point. On the compass, the quest givers at proximity are shown by a white exclamation mark.

Starving Hunter?

By the way, inhabitants of your village can also have some quests for you. Their quest are often based on their profession but don't indicate the current situation of your village. The hunter who regularly hunts 30 pieces of meat for your village will ask for help because his family is starving. Don't worry, the quest and his efficiency have nothing to do with each other.

At first, you can speak with the quest givers, find out what they need or want and then decide whether you want to help them or not. You can accept their quest later or just refuse without any negative consequence. When the season changes, these quests will disappear and new ones will appear.

If you accept a quest, you have to complete it within the season or it is considered as failed. Some quests have further conditions (e.g., only possible during the night) which you can see in the quest description of your *Journal* (key J / ⊚ / Ⓒⓡ).

Most quest tasks are to obtain tools, resources, hunting specific animals or to deliver a message or an item to an inhabitant of an other village.

Challenges/ The King

Last but not least, another person who needs your help is the *King*. His *Herald* appears randomly in a village with a tavern (it can also be in your village if you have a tavern!).

You know the herald is in the valley when you can see the ceremonial trumpet icon on the map and on the compass. The compass always indicates the trumpet, no matter how far away the herald is.

You also recognize the herald easily by the superior quality of his clothes. When you speak with him, you can learn more about the king and his opinion of you. Furthermore, the herald is looking for help on behalf of the king. You can listen to his request and then decide if you want to help him.

If you succeed, not only will you get a profitable reward for your effort, but you will also gain a better reputation with the king. Apart from the dynasty reputation you get, your good reputation will decrease your taxes.

But beware! This can be a double-edged sword: If the king is good, your reputation increases, and with it the satisfaction among the inhabitants of your village. However, if the king is bad or evil, your reputation with the king increases, but it decreases with the common people and you receive minus points on the satisfaction of your inhabitants.

You can tell if a king is good, neutral or bad by looking at his name. You get all the important information about the current king and the bonuses and minus points you already have on the *Map* (key *M* /  / Ctrl):

Stefan I the Greedy   Good (-10% , -2%)

On the picture above, we have already fulfilled 2 quests for our King, *Stefan I the Greedy*. (You can see it in your *Journal* by pressing the key *J* / ⊚ / Ctrl). That's why our standing with the king is *Good* and we have a tax bonus of *-10%* (=-10% less taxes to pay). However, the satisfaction of our inhabitants is decreasing by *2%* because we are supporting a bad king.

Good and beloved kings

Fulfilling the quest:

> Decreases the annual taxes
> Increases the satisfaction of your inhabitants

Failing of the quest:

> Increases the annual taxes as a punishment
> Decreases the satisfaction of your inhabitants

Typical bynames of good kings: the Merciful, the Builder, the Beloved, the Wise, the Caring, the Fair, ...

Neutral and ignored kings:

Fulfilling the quest:

> Decreases the annual taxes

Failing of the quest:

> Increases the tax as a punishment

Typical bynames of neutral kings: the Great, the Strong, the Lion, the Lazy, the Coward, ...

Bad and hated kings:

Fulfilling the quest:

> Decreases the annual taxes
> Decreases the satisfaction of your inhabitants

Failing of the quest:

> Increases the annual taxes as a punishment
> Increases the satisfaction of your inhabitants

Typical bynames of bad kings: the Dangerous, the Greedy, the Warlike, the Mad, the Cruel, the Aggressor, ...

The amount of bonuses and minus points depends on the king. They also increase or decrease by fulfilling or failing challenges. There are 3 levels of negative or positive reputation you can have with each king. You can confidently refuse tasks or not go to the herald at all, this will not disadvantage you. Only the failure of a challenge will bring you negative reputation.

There are various kinds of challenges but you clearly will need more resources to fulfill these tasks than for other quests. For example, you have to recruit 3 people for the king, hunt 30 boars or wolves or donate 1500 coins for a wedding.

Too Many Items Demanded?

The exact amount, for example of coins, is only indicated in the journal after having accepted the challenge. That's why you should save the game before, so that you have the possibility to refuse the challenge.

The king can die at any season change:

» The older he is, the higher the probability he dies

» The more challenges you fail, the higher the probability of his death

» Successful challenges increase his survival probability

The king is dead – long live the king: another king is chosen immediately by chance after the death of his predecessor and your reputation with the king and the mood of your inhabitants is set to 0 again.

Events

Next to quests and tasks, there are also random events. At the end of a season, a random event can occur, sometimes related to a specific season. You cannot stop these random events and sometimes you have the choice between 2 or 3 possibilities which influence the ending of the event. The option of choosing often depends on your skill level of a skill tree.

The possible events are:

War Taxes

The Kingdom is preparing for war. According to the King's decree, taxes are being raised. Hopefully, tensions will fall soon, and those demands won't last that long.

I hate taxes...
Taxes increase by 20%

Surely the king can give us some pardon...
Taxes increase by 10%
- 500 Dynasty Reputation.
(Dynasty Reputation at least 3000)

Send a letter to the king.
Taxes increased by 15%.
(diplomacy at least 7)

I'm not paying that!
-1000 Dynasty Reputation.

Dangerous Storm

Some sudden and very strong storm has passed through your village during the night and damaged some of your buildings. Thankfully no one was hurt.

Accept
(2-8) buildings get (5%-60%) damage

The Night is Dark and Full of Howls

During the night there was a terrifying howl heard in every corner of our village. No one has felt safe since then. Hopefully, the animals won't come any closer to the village.

Hide under the bed.
All villagers lose 25 mood

Comfort people.
All villagers gain 5 mood
(diplomacy at least 5)

Kingdom for a Scarecrow!

Some hungry birds took the opportunity when nobody was watching and decided to have a feast.

Accept
(1-4) fields get (2%-60%) damaged

Fever Night

There's a fever spreading in your town. A lot of your inhabitants are lying sick and those who are not are afraid to catch the disease.

Let them rest
(90%-100%) of the villagers work 25% less efficient.

Give them some herbs
(5%-15%) of the villagers work 25% less efficient.
-10 x Broadleaf Plantain

Thief

A thief was caught red-handed while trying to steal your resources. He tries to make excuses and convince you that he did this because of poverty. Now it's up to you to decide what to do with him.

Cut his hands off.
All villagers lose 10 mood
-50 Dynasty Reputation

Let him go and banish him.
(1%-5%) of crafting items get removed from storages

Order someone to cut his hands off.
All villagers lose 20 mood

Knowledge is Power

A mysterious man came to your village. He claims that he knows a lot about wilderness and can teach you some new skills for some golden coins.

Decline

Question of survival
500 skill points in: survival
-1000 coins
(survival max. 4, 1000 coins)

Ask about hunting
500 skill points in: hunting
-1000 coins
(hunting max. 4, 1000 coins)

Show him that you know more.
+250 coins
(hunting and survival at least 5)

Medieval Dynasty

Man in Tights

A nobleman was passing through your village. He lost his purse in front of you. What will you do?

Return it to the nobleman.
+100 Dynasty Reputation
All villagers lose 5 mood

Let your people have it
All villagers gain 10 mood

Take it for yourself.
+100 coins
All villagers lose 15 mood

Heavy Rain

A heavy rainfall flooded some of your fields. A few of your crops have gone to waste in the process. Thankfully, the weather seems to be stable now.

Accept
(3-9) fields get (10%-70%) damage.

Medieval Dynasty

Rainbow in the Sky

There's a beautiful rainbow after the rain. It looks nice. Your people seem happy, and they consider it for a good omen.

Accept
All villagers gain 10 mood

Slew of Inspiration

You feel inspired! You want to encourage your people to work harder. You could deliver a speech, which should put them in the right spirit. However a poor one may have a discouraging effect.

Deliver a speech.
All villagers work 15% more efficient.

Deliver an inspiring speech!
All villagers work 30% more efficient.
(Diplomatie >= 5)

Maybe it's not such a good idea...

Plague of Vermin

The rats ate some of your food from the food storage. One can never truly get rid of them, can they?

Accept
(5%-10%) of consumables got removed from storages

Scorching Sun

The temperature is incredibly high this Summer. You can barely breathe in this heat. You should carry water with you at all times just in case.

Accept
Water decreases (10%-70%) faster.
Stamina decreases (10%-70%) faster.

The Black Clouds

The weather is very depressing. The sun was not out for days. This will affect your people.

> **Accept**
> All villagers lose 10 mood.

The Boy who cried Wolf

A boy runs screaming into your town. He claims to have seen twenty wolves in the woods nearby. Your villagers are starting to get nervous. "That's a lot of wolves", one said.

> **Shoo the kid away.**
> (20%-60%) villagers work 45 %less efficient.

> **Try talking with your people.**
> (20%-60%) villagers work 20% less efficient.
> *(diplomacy at least 2)*

> **Say you will kill them if need be.**
> +(5-10) Dynasty Reputation
> +6 Meat
> +5 Fur
> *(hunting at least 5, survival at least3)*

> **Say you will lay some traps.**
> (10%-50%) work 10% less efficient.
> *(crafting at least 3)*

Golden Autumn

The weather is really nice this Autumn. Pretty leaves falling from trees. It's a great time to get something done!

> **Accept**
> Water decreases (50%-5%) slower.
> Stamina decreases (50%-5%) slower.

Moody Villagers

Due to bad mood of your villagers productivity is down. No one wants to work!

> **They'll get over it.**
> All villagers work 45% less efficient.

> **Try talking to them**
> All villagers work 20% less efficient.
> *(diplomacy at least 2)*

> **Drinks are on me!**
> All villagers work 5% less efficient.
> -50 x Coin
> *(50 coins, at least 1 tavern)*

Harsh Winds

Strong winds damaged some of your buildings. Thankfully no one was hurt.

> **Accept**
> (3-9) Buildings get (2%-40%) damage.

News of War

News spread around the land that a war has broken out between our neighbouring country and their enemies... Let us hope we don't have to get involved...

> **This might increase the prices of some goods...**
> All villagers lose 1 mood.

> **Poor bastards.**
> All villagers lose 1 mood.

> **Hey, as long as I'm not involved, I don't care.**
> All villagers lose 1 mood.

Harsh Winds

Strong gusts of wind caused some of your inhabitants to get hurt. They won't be able to work normally for some time.

Accept
(2%-20%) of your villagers work 15% less efficient.

Help your people
(survival at least 5)

Traveling Merchant

A traveling merchant is visiting your settlement. He presents you his wares, and tells stories about faraway lands he saw. For a proper price, he can teach you a few tricks about haggling.

Sure I could use some advice.
+500 diplomacy points
(200 coins, diplomacy max. 9)

Show him that you know more.
+1500 coins
(diplomacy at least 10)

Decline politely

Winter of the Century

It's so c-c-c-cold... It won't be easy to work in these conditions.

Accept
All villagers work 30% less efficient.

Wedding Day

You and your inhabitants have been invited to a wedding! Everyone will attend the ceremony and have a jolly good time.

A toast to the couple!
All villagers gain 15 mood.

Let's celebrate the whole night!
All villagers gain 30 mood.
(at least 1 tavern)

Hunting Incident

The king and his hunting party had their annual hunt in the forests nearby. Such a prestigious event was however cut short due to an unfortunate accident. One of your villagers was shot with an arrow by one of the king's men who mistook them for a deer. The King extended his apology for the recklessness of his man and offered a compensation for the damages.

Thank you my Lord
1 of the villagers works 3% less efficient.
+200 coins

Spring Blooms

Spring is right around the corner and the sight of green trees and blooming flowers is filling everyone's hearts with joy!

That's a good way to start a season!
All villagers gain 15 mood.

2.7 Bandits

Bandit Camps

Whilst traveling, you will sometimes find yourself face to face with bandit camps. The outlaws attack you immediately trying to kill you and steal your belongings! Often, these camps are near roads and paths. Sometimes, they are also a bit more remote.

Whether they actually show up, their location and the exact amount of bandits spawned on the map depends on the season. Over time, there are more and more bandit camps.

There are camps with 1 to 5 bandits and they can be armed with various weapons:

» **Archer:** very dangerous due to his long attack range. He also has close combat weapons.

» **Crossbowman:** just as dangerous, if not more. Drops good loot, though.

» **Spearman:** with his spear, he causes lots of damage.

» **Axeman:** even if he can cause lots of damage with his axe, he can't attack as fast as the spearman!

» **Batman:** this highwayman is faster with the cudgel than an axeman and causes less damage, you still shouldn't underestimate him!

» **Cutthroat:** this bandit only has a knife. Fast but only low damage.

» **Bruiser:** a poor blighter and unarmed. If you're armed and have all your health points, this opponent shouldn't be a problem.

Fighting Tactics

You should always carry a long-distance weapon (bow / crossbow) and a close combat weapon (preferably spears) with you. You should also have 2-4 healing potions on you, as soon as you can make them.

If you get into an unexpected fight and get injured, you can open your inventory anytime (by pressing **I** 🔘 / **Ctrl**) and heal yourself instantly with the healing potions!

Your fighting tactic should mainly be based on your equipment:

Unarmed:

Run! You shouldn't pick a fight with armed bandits. If you flee, the bandits will follow you for some time, but then give up and go back to their camp.

If bandits with bows and crossbows follow you, try to zigzag and take cover behind trees and hills.

Close combat fight:

During a close combat fight, you should keep yourself occupied with one bandit at a time. Run away a bit, until only one bandit follows you. Kill him and heal yourself with healing potions, then take care of the next one.

Long distance fight:

The best way to kill a pack of bandits is with a bow or crossbow. A single headshot with a bow and an iron arrow is often already enough. With crossbows, aiming is a lot easier while running! You want to shoot fast? Then choose the recurve bow!

Always kill the bowmen first, since they are the most dangerous!

The tactic of running away is also helpful during a long-distance fight, until you have a single bandit left. When bandits turn around to go back to their camp, you can stab them in the back easily. Not honorable? – When it comes down to it, we are not an honorable knight!

Loot

Bandits can be very annoying but they offer good loot and Dynasty Reputation, when you kill them:

» In their camps, you can find torches, tools, weapons, arrows, bolts, backpacks, beverages, food and even more.

» In the camps, pay attention to bags and chests you can open! And don't overlook small coin bags, which are often hard to see on the brown ground.

» Bandits attack you, as soon as they notice you, but they always have a camp. Find it by searching in the direction from which the bandits came.

» You can also plunder the bandits. Most of the time, you find their weapons, some food, alcohol and a few coins. Especially the archers and the crossbowmen offer you much loot as well as a rich supply of arrows and bolts!

Medieval Dynasty

Possible Locations

The possible locations of the bandit camps are fixed, but the bandits themselves appear randomly at some of these places at every change of a season. If you're on the road by night or if the weather's bad, look for the light of the campfires.

On the map below, you see the most probable spots of bandit camps. They are mostly near the roads, so that they notice you when you pass by. With the game updates since version 1.0, so many new locations were added that drawing them would make the map unreadable!

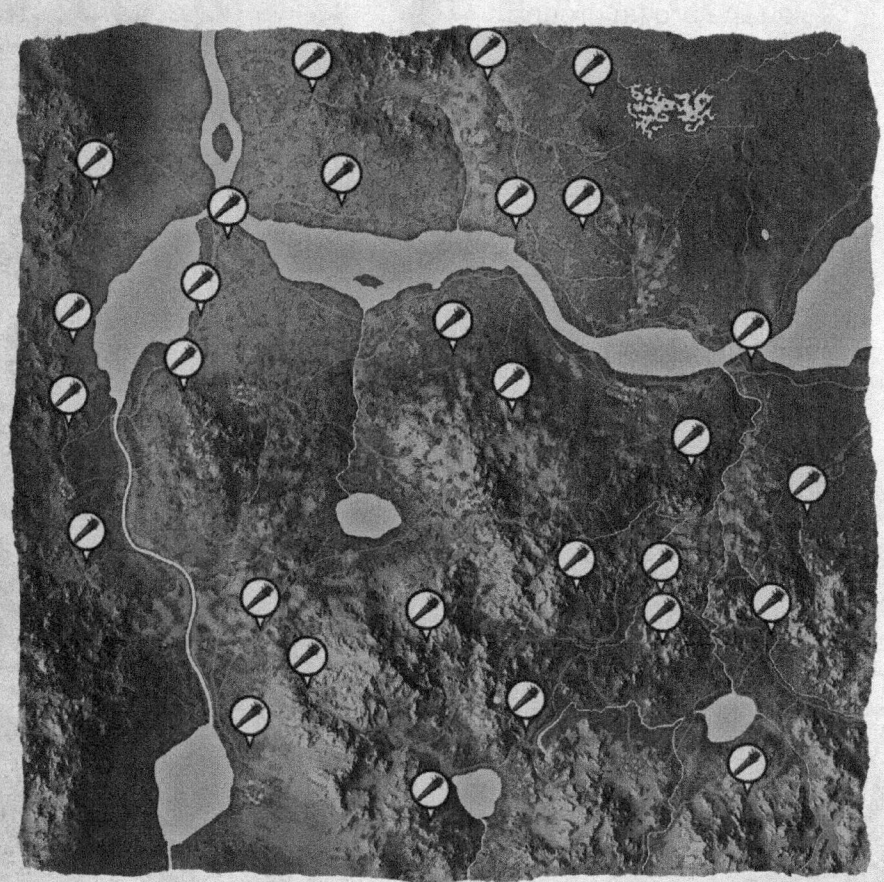

HAHA! Bandit scum! Who plunders who now?

These bandits pitched their camp near the road leading to Lesnica:

3 Building and Crafting

h, I see you noticed my hammer- well, you're surely wondering, why I display it this way, on its own pedestal carved out of oak wood. It deserves a place of honor! You know, this hammer made all the hamlets here - well, that's perhaps slightly exaggerated, but less than you would think.

We aren't in the city or in one of the big villages with their own craftsmen. Oh yes, we have able blacksmiths, gifted bow makers and seamstresses, who sew your handy attire for you - but, frequently you have to grasp the tools yourself and create with your own hand strength what you need to live. This holds true for a barn as well as for the bowl of soup you're slurping now! It's good, isn't it? I sowed the beetroots myself, my daughter harvested them and the salt comes from the mountains here. I added a piece of lard, let it simmer and now, it's a meal to be proud of. Makes you as strong as an ox!

But I'm digressing from the hammer. I carpentered my first modest dwelling with it, decades after my uncle did the same before me. My old uncle, whom I never met, but about whom the whole valley is gossiping. One of the tales is the story of how he got this hammer.

At that time, you weren't even thought of yet and I still was a small rascal down by the see, he earned a modest fortune as a river and coastal skipper. During spring, from Hamburg to Prague and back again, in summer alongside the seashore and in early autumn from Gdansk back to Plock, where he spent the winter. On a mild may morning, he had left Dresden behind him with a hefty load of merchandise - and a passenger. A carpenter, at least he passed himself off as such. On the first day, he was harmless, on the second day, he began to ask questions concerning type and value of the merchandise, which didn't appease my uncle at all. On the fourth day, they got dragged into rough waters, surging from the rain, and a plank was ripped off my uncles boat by a fallen tree from the shoreline.

No real harm done, not enough, to make them halt their journey and commission repairs in the next city. Nay, my uncle had wood and nails on board, presented both to his passenger and instructed him to mend the damages. Ha, how clumsy he was! He missed the nail again and again and even hit his own fingers thrice. After the third time, my uncle held one of the swords onboard, destined for the city guards of Prague, under his nose. He forced him to put his cards on the table and accused him of stealing the hammer and of being a scoundrel, who only had it in for the load.

He didn't even deny it, jumped back and grabbed the few goods and chattels, he could snatch before leaping over board and fighting himself to shore. Not a big loss for my uncle, and he kept the hammer. I inherited it and my grandson will use it next to raise a house.

3 Building and crafting

Crafting objects and erecting buildings represent a large part of the game. For this reason, we want to take a closer look at these 2 activities:

3.1 Crafting Objects

You can craft objects by yourself or, as soon as you have your own village with inhabitants and the appropriate production buildings, let your inhabitants produce them for you.

Do it Yourself

You can craft simple objects at anytime in your creation menu. The following requirements are necessary:

» You already bought the corresponding scheme.

» You have the required resources in your inventory.

Then open the building menu (key by default: *Q* / RB / R1)

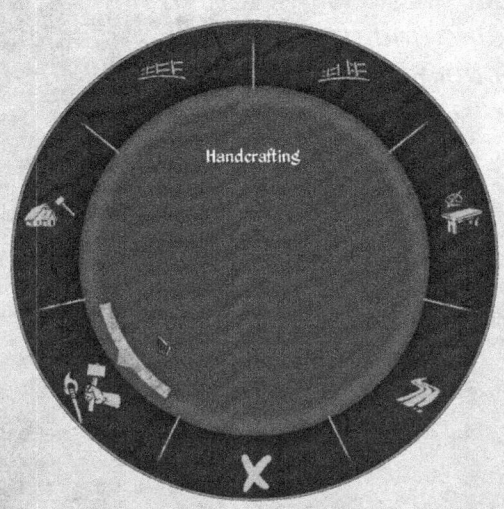

Move the cursor over *Handcrafting* and select it.

To manufacture an object, move the cursor on the item and select it, if you want to make more of them at once, press *R* / Ⓨ / △ :

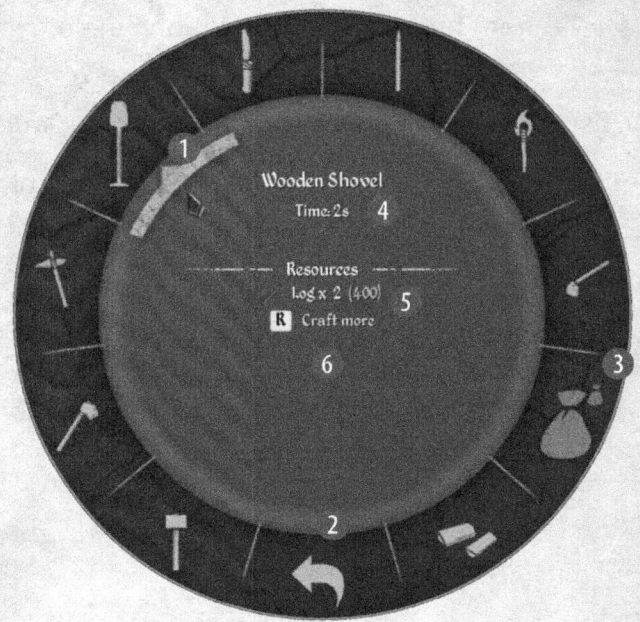

1 Selection of the item.

2 Back to the previous menu.

3 Red bag: not enough resources to craft the object.

4 Name of the item and required crafting time.

5 Necessary resources (between the brackets, you can see the amount you have in your inventory).

6 Additional information: e.g., press *R* / Ⓨ / △ to craft more objects at the same time.

Building at stations

More advanced items have to be produced at crafting stations. The requirements for this are:

» The required building with the crafting station (e.g., workshop, smithy or kitchen) has been built (stations in somebody else's station can't be used!).

» The corresponding scheme has been unlocked (bought).

» The required resources are in the inventory of the player.

Building Tiers

Some crafting stations are only available in the higher tiers of buildings. E.g., *Workshop I* only possesses the *Workbench*. The *Potter Wheel* for clay wares is only available from *Workshop II* upwards *!*

A smithy III with workbench, forge and anvil.

Go to a crafting station (e.g., forge or stove), look at it and press the indicated key to open the creation menu (E / Ⓐ / ⓧ). In the image below, you can see the anvil.

Select the desired object category (example below: copper tools). These subdivisions into different categories are not available at every station.

Then, you can craft the object by selecting it. As ever, you can craft several items at once by pressing *R* / Ⓨ / △ .

The display of the creation menu of a station is the same as the creation menu of the player. In addition, you can see:

1 A blue padlock: the scheme for the item has not been bought yet.

2 If the scheme is available, you can buy it directly here and don't need to go to the *Technology Menu*. Press *R* / Ⓨ / △ to buy the scheme (provided the scheme is available and that you have enough coins).

Let It Be Produced

Of course, it is more comfortable to have your inhabitants collect the needed resources and craft the objects you want by themselves.

To do this you need to follow these steps:

» An available inhabitant.

» The suitable production building is already built.

» In the *Management Display Screen* the inhabitant is assigned to the building as a worker.

» The required tools (e.g., a hammer for a workshop) have been placed into *Building's Chest* or into its *Resource Storage* and the required resources are available.

» The production we want to be done in the building is allocated in the *Management Display Screen* in *Assignments*.

If all these conditions are fulfilled, the selected amount will be produced every day as long as the required tools and resources are available.

Controlling the Production

Open the management display screen (key *N* / ⊚ / 🎮) from time to time and select the house overview. If there is a problem and nothing is being produced, you will see a red icon at the status in the list. The tool could be broken and no other tool is available, a type of resource could be completely depleted, or the only female worker of that building could have had a baby and, therefore, will not be able to work for the next two years.

Assigning a person to a production building

To assign an inhabitant to a production building, open the *Management Display Screen* (*N* / ⊗ / Ctrl).

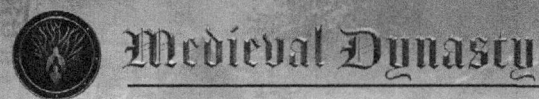

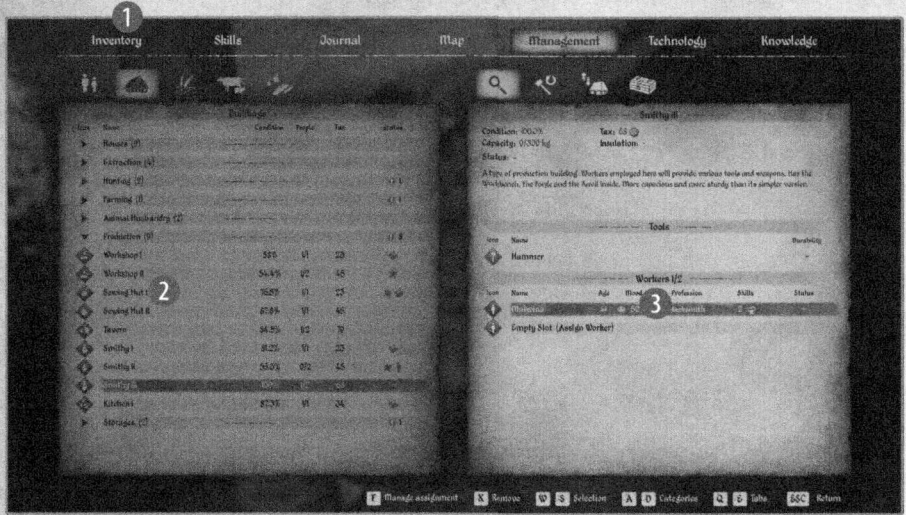

1. Choose the building administration.

2. Open the desired building with a *double-click* or press *F* / Ⓐ / ⊗. You can now see the details in the right panel.

3. Select an empty slot or on an assigned slot, if you want to exchange the worker. Then you can choose the desired inhabitant.

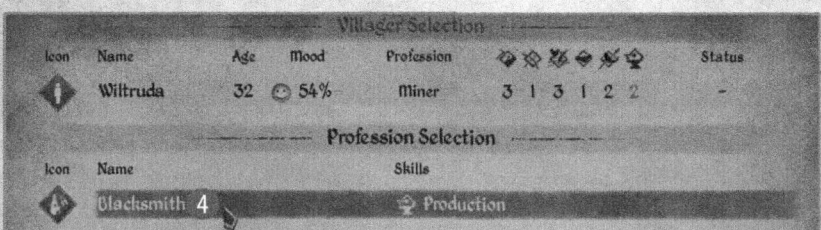

4. **Important:** To definitely assign the worker, you must select the name of the profession once more.

In the status window of the building administration, you have a general overview.

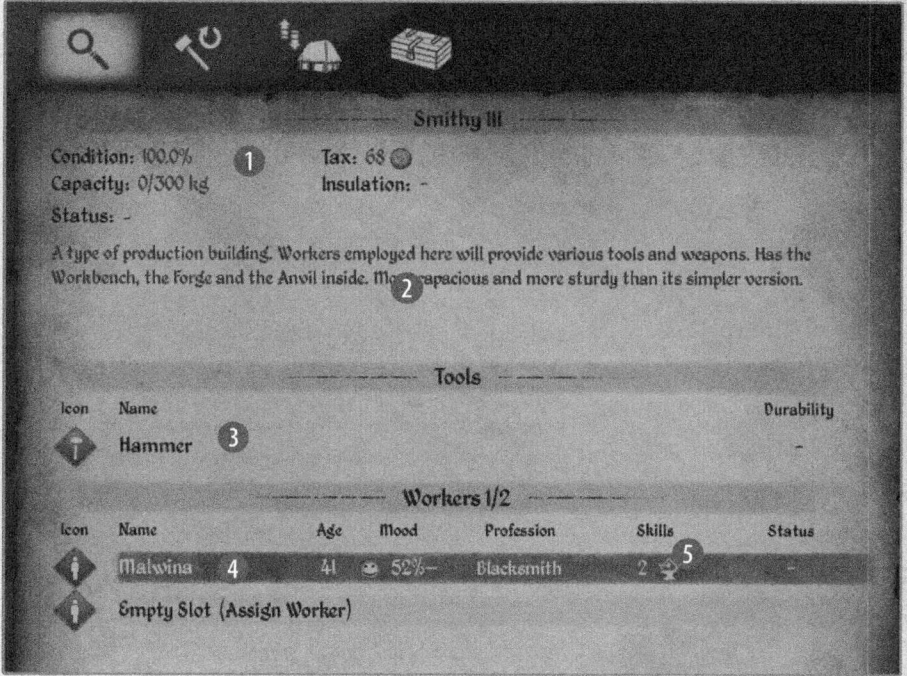

Condition: 100.0%   **1**   Tax: 68
Capacity: 0/300 kg   Insulation: -
Status: -

A type of production building. Workers employed here will provide various tools and weapons. Has the Workbench, the Forge and the Anvil inside. M**2**apacious and more sturdy than its simpler version.

---------- Tools ----------

Icon	Name						Durability
🔨	Hammer **3**						-

---------- Workers 1/2 ----------

Icon	Name	Age	Mood	Profession	Skills	Status
👤	Malwina **4**	41	52%–	Blacksmith	2 **5**	-
👤	Empty Slot (Assign Worker)					

1 Condition of the building, the annual tax price of the building and the capacity of the chest.

2 A description of the building.

3 The required tools for the inhabitants to work in the building (the tools have to be stowed in the local chest or in the resource storage).

4 The assigned workers and their values.

5 The applied skill of the worker is displayed here (the higher it is, the faster the production!).

Assigning tasks

When you have assigned an inhabitant to a building and there are enough tools and resources available in the chest or in the resource storage, you can allocate the work assignments. Open the building administration (*N* / ⊚ / Cr) and select a building:

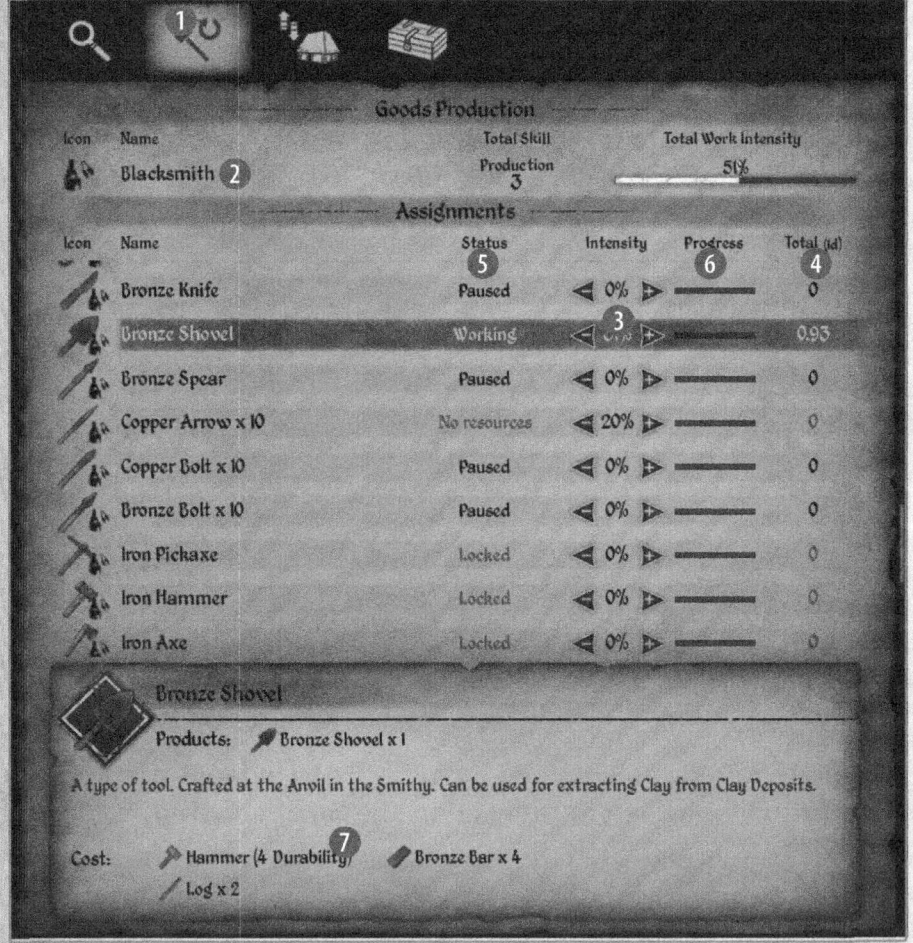

① Select this icon to open the assignment list.

2 In this area, you can see the profession's name and the total skill of all the assigned workers. The higher the value, the faster they will produce (more items per day). The % indication shows, to which extent the workers are occupied.

3 With the *arrows* / Ⓐ & Ⓧ / Ⓧ & ⬜ you can adapt the work intensity for the selected object. The higher the value, the more of this item will be produced.

4 In this column, the daily production amount is indicated. Decimal places are also taken into account. For example, if 1.2 is indicated, 6 items are produced in 5 days (5 x 1.2).

5 In the status column, you can see the current production. *Working* written in green indicates that the item is being produced. *Paused* means, that the work intensity is set to 0. Red writing means that, due to a missing requirement, nothing is being produced: *No resources* or *No tool* available or the scheme hasn't been bought yet (*Locked*). The production also stops when the workers have their *Free time* or when they can't produce it in the current season (*Invalid Season*).

6 In the progress column, you can see the production progress of the current day.

7 By selecting a tool, a description window opens at the bottom of the screen, also indicating the required resources to produce this item.

You can also assign a job to a worker in the people overview. Select an inhabitant in the people overview and assign him or her to a profession in the same way as described above for the production buildings! There is no other option for assignment management!

Schemes

For most tools, weapons and objects, you must buy the required scheme first. Otherwise, you or your inhabitants cannot craft these items.

Schemes can be bought in the *Technology Tree* of the respective building.

Open the Technology display screen with *T* / ◉ / Cr :

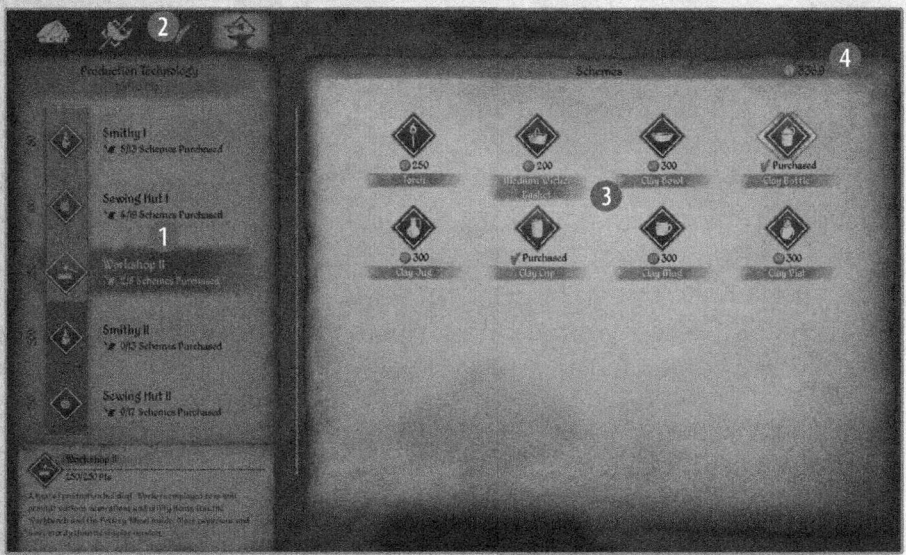

Select one of the buildings on the left side ❶ of one of the four technology categories ❷.

On the right ❸, you can see the schemes you can unlock for the chosen building. If you have enough money ❹, you can buy a scheme with a *double-click* or the key Ⓐ / ⊗ . You can also buy these schemes in the creation menu wheel, if available.

Tips regarding schemes

» You can unlock the first schemes quickly, since you only need a bit of technology experience. For example, hunt some wild animals to receive 50 experience points and unlock the *Hunting Lodge* in *Survival Technology* in order to unlock the schemes for a simple *Bow* and *Stone Arrows*. You can also progress quickly in the first levels of the other technologies by just performing the corresponding activities.

» Only buy the schemes you really need and not all of them. You can craft *Stone Knifes* quickly and sell them for 15 coins each. Like this, you rapidly gain the required amount of money to unlock the schemes you want.

» Also consider the required resources to craft an object. For example, you can easily buy the scheme for a *Bucket* (10 experience points in crafting technology for 100 coins). But to produce a bucket, you need *Planks*, which you can only craft in the *Woodshed* (100 experience points in the building technology). Or you have to buy or steel planks.

3.2 Constructing Buildings

To construct a building, you need the appropriate raw materials in your inventory and to expand or repair the building you must also equip a hammer.

First, you define the building site of your house, this costs you nothing.

Open the *creation menu* with the key *Q* / RB / R1:

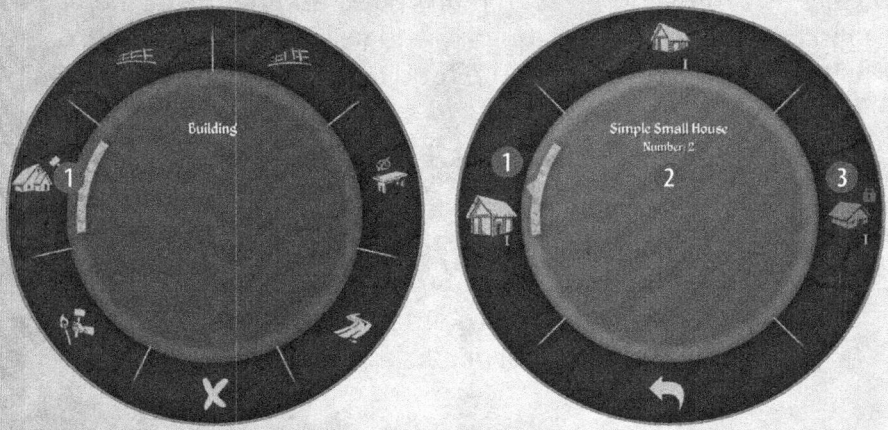

1 Select the building category and then the desired house.

2 In the middle of the creation menu, you can see how many buildings of this type you have already built.

3 Unavailable buildings are marked with a blue padlock. Move your cursor over the building and in the center 2 will appear the amount of experience points required in the corresponding technology tree.

The framing of the house will then be shown in the game. If it's green, you can place it there, but if it's red, something is blocking the construction (e.g., a road, a tree, uneven terrain, or you're too close to another village, etc..). The reason why you cannot construct your house is shown in yellow under the construction display.

Swing the hammer and the building site is ready:

Use the hammer to build the foundation. The required amount of logs or stones is displayed in the center of the screen. The type of foundation is automatically determined when you select the building site. On straight surfaces, a stone foundation is built. For some buildings, on sloping surfaces, a wooden foundation is built.

Then use the hammer on the blue displayed bars of the framing (see picture previous page below) to finish it (picture above). The cost of this is again displayed in the center of the screen.

Now you have to build the walls and the roof.

To do this, the required raw materials also must be in your inventory. If you are building a house, you can determine the type of walls and roof (see next sub-chapter). For all the other buildings, the type of walls and roof will be determined by the level of the building.

There are 3 different walls:

> › Level 1: wattle wall made of sticks.
> › Level 2: wooden wall made of logs.
> › Level 3: stone wall made of stones.

There are 3 roof types:

> › Level 1: thatch roof made of straw.
> › Level 2: wooden roof made of planks.
> › Level 3: wooden tile roof made of planks.

Heat Insulation Decreases Heating Costs!

The better the quality of the walls and roof, the less firewood your inhabitants need, as the insulation is better. The houses also become more stable, the higher the quality of the walls and roof. They do not deteriorate so quickly then.

Now, equip the *Hammer* and aim at a wall. Swing it until the wall (or the roof) is constructed. Repeat this until all walls, the roof, inside walls and, if available, the attic are built. Consider that you could have to enter into the house to build the inside walls and the attic.

The building is finished, when all walls, the roof and the inside walls are completed. Then, the furnishing, like *Workbenches*, *Fireplaces* and *Beds*, will appear automatically in the building.

Medieval Dynasty

Houses

You can build every house differently. You can change every single wall and build it out of the material you want.

After having built the framing, equip a *Hammer*. The unfinished walls are displayed in light-blue. Walls you already started building are indicated in light-green. Approach one of the walls, aim at it with the hammer and press *E* / Ⓐ / ⊗. A creation menu will appear, where you can change the type of the wall and out of which material it is made:

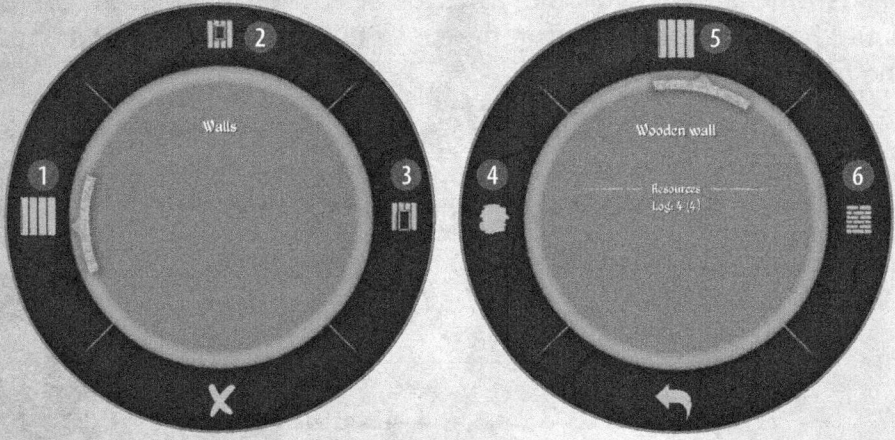

» You first choose between a normal wall ①, a wall with a window ② or a wall with door ③.

» Then you choose if the wall should be made of wickerwork ④, wood ⑤ or stone ⑥.

In the same way, you choose if the roof should be made of reed (straw), planks or shingles.

You can relocate doors, windows and normal walls as desired and give each house an individual touch. The interior furnishing will be adapted automatically. A house can only have one door.

Additionally, you can plaster the walls with the *Right Mouse Button* / LT / L2 while using the *Hammer*. Select the *Upgrade* mode and then use the hammer on the walls.

Requirement: you have unlocked the level 2 ability *Handyman* in the *Production Skill Tree*.

You can plaster wickerwork and wood walls with *Daub*. You can buy the scheme for daub at the *Barn* in the *Farming technology* for 50 coins. You need 10 *Straw* and 10 *Clay* to produce daub at the *Workbench* of the Barn or you can buy it from vendors without buying the scheme. You can also buy the *Daub* without a scheme.

To plaster stone walls, you need *Limestone*. You can get limestone while using the *Pickaxe* on rocks, or in *Caves*. You can use limestone directly on walls without further processing it.

Higher quality walls and roofs bring the following advantages:

> The house receives less damage during an event.
> The inhabitants' mood increases.
> The inhabitants need less firewood.

The best houses are stone houses, plastered with limestone, and with wooden tile roofs.

Here, you can see the 3 types of wall with their plastering.

Quality Pays Off!

At the beginning of the game, it's a lot easier to find sticks for wattle walls than stones for stone walls. We still recommend to make all your residential houses of stone and to plaster them with limestone as soon as possible.

It's true that you can later destroy the wattle walls and replace them with stone walls, but this costs you an unnecessary amount of time and resources. High quality buildings from the start save a lot of time and money in the long run.

Further Buildings

All other buildings are built in the exact same way as houses, apart from the fact that you can't adapt walls or windows. You can also plaster them.

Storage buildings

There are 2 storage buildings:

> Food storage: for food and beverages

> Resource storage: for everything else (tools, raw materials, seeds, weapons, objects etc.)

Storage buildings replace the chests in the houses. You won't need to put food, water and firewood in every house to supply your inhabitants with these resources. They will take what they need from the storage buildings by themselves. This also applies to all tools and resources. These will only have to be placed in the resource storage and not in the corresponding production buildings anymore.

If you possess more than one storage building of a type, their content will add up. All the storages of one type share a common inventory.

Example:

You have one *Resource Storage I* (1000kg storage capacity) and two *Resource Storages II* (2000kg storage capacity each). Then you have the same inventory in all your resource storages with a total of 5000kg storage capacity.

> Use this to your advantage! You can ,e.g., build a resource storage near a different village. You will then be able to comfortably take objects out of your storage from it, without having to run straight across the map to a possibly far away village.

Exploitation buildings

These buildings are meant to extract raw materials. You can assign inhabitants to these buildings and they will collect the corresponding raw materials. In some of these buildings, there are workbenches to process them further. These buildings are listed below:

» Well: buckets of water and full waterskins

» Woodshed: logs and sticks

» Excavation shed: stones and clay

» Mine: stones and ores (iron too!)

» Hunting lodge: meat, leather, feathers and pelt

» Fishing hut: fish

» Herbalist's hut: herbs, berries and mushrooms

Farming buildings

» Barn: sowing, harvesting and further processing of grains

» Windmill: grinds as many grains as the barn but produces twice as much flour!

» All stables: to accommodate the corresponding animals

Production buildings

Only raw materials are processed in the production buildings:

» Workshop: clay and wood products

» Kitchen: food

» Smithy: metal products, tools and weapons

» Sewing hut: hats, clothes, shoes

» Tavern: beverages

3.3 Repairing or Demolishing a Building

Buildings are damaged through time or because of events. To see damaged elements, you have to use the hammer. Use the *Right Mouse Click* / LT / L2 and select the *Repair* mode.

Now you are able to see the damaged buildings:

Red elements (see image above) have a durability of less than 50% and need to be repaired. Elements in a better condition than 50% can't be repaired (green).

You will need the required raw materials in your inventory to repair the current wall or roof *(sticks, logs, stones, straw, planks)*. Then, use the hammer in the repair mode on the wall or the roof until it is restored to 100%.

The better the quality of the house, the less it will be damaged over time and the less time you have to invest in repairing the buildings!

Automatic repair

Of course, the most comfortable way of repairing buildings is letting your villagers repair them. To do this you have to build a *Builder's Hut* (only available at 7500 XP in the Building Technology).

Assign a worker to the hut (builder), as you did for the other buildings (see chapter 3.1 Assigning a person to a production building). Open the *Management Display Screen* (*N* / ⊚ / Ctrl), select the list of buildings at the top left and open the builder's hut with a *double-click* / Ⓐ / ⊗. The detail overview appears on the right side of the screen:

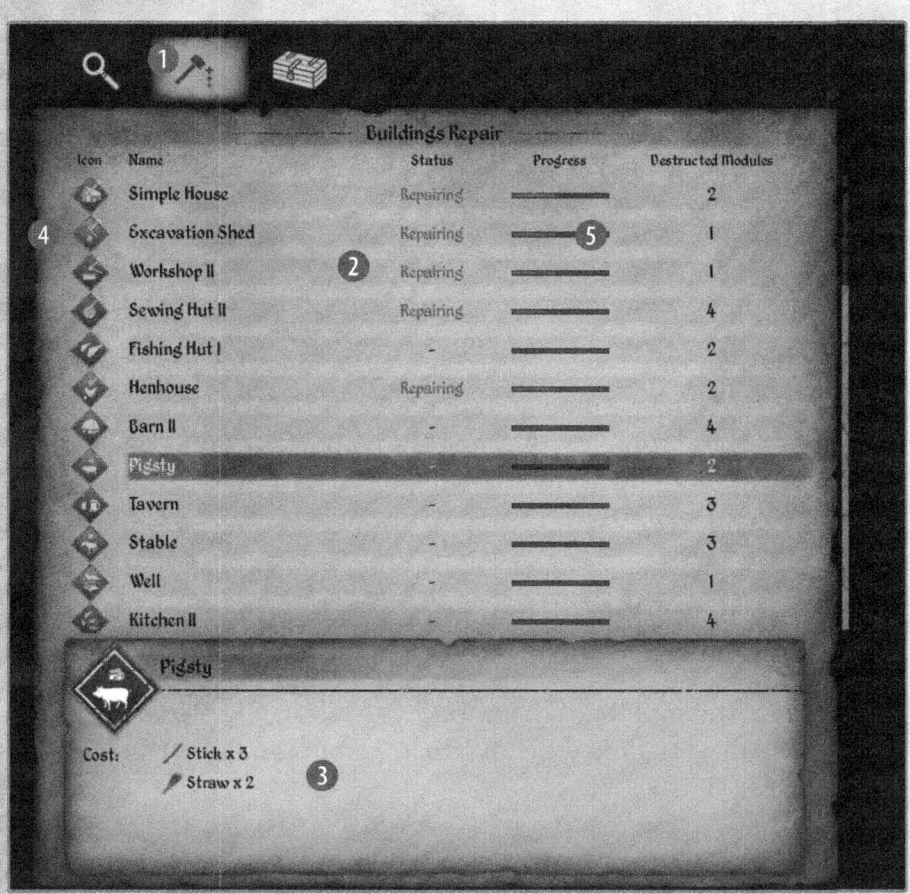

In the detail overview, you see the required tools and assigned villagers. In the top bar, select *Buildings Repair* ❶ to switch to this window.

In this list, you see all damaged buildings ❷. Choose one of them to see the materials required to repair it ❸. Select a building (*double-click* / Ⓐ / ⊗) to have it repaired. You recognize the buildings you already selected by the small green hammer in the icon ❹.

For a builder to repair buildings, a *Hammer* and the required materials need to be in the *Resource Storage* or in the chest of the builder's hut.

You see the repairing progress ❺ in the progress bar. A building that has been repaired disappears from the list.

Destroying a building

» Select the *Hammer* and choose the *Destroy* mode with the *Right Mouse Button* / LT / L2 .

» Now use the hammer on the walls and roofs you want to destroy.

» Once all the walls and roofs are destroyed, only the building's framing and foundation are left.

» Now, you can destroy the framing and the foundation as well and the building will no longer exist.

> You can't destroy a framing before the chest of the building is empty! In this way, you can't delete items accidentally.

With this method, you can also destroy walls and roofs of houses and build them up again using a different material.

If you have unlocked the level 1 skill *Master of Destruction* of the skill tree *Extraction*, you will get back 50% of the raw materials of an element you're destroying.

3.4   Upgrading a Building

Many buildings come in several levels, such as the barn of levels I, II and III. The higher the level, the better the materials used in construction (e.g. wattle, wooden log or stone). Likewise, you often get more workplaces and more crafting facilities.

When you unlock a new upgrade level, you can build that building, but then you may have two buildings of the same type. Therefore you can upgrade existing buildings (except for residential houses).

Select the building of the new level in the construction menu. Now aim at the already existing building of the lower level and place the new building so that they overlap exactly and then swing the hammer.

All you have to do now is upgrade the walls, roof and ceilings and the building has been upgraded to the new level. However, you have to reassign all workers and also redefine the work tasks. These are not automatically taken over. The content of chests remains unaffected by the improvement!

3.5   Decorating buildings

Interiors embellishment

Since the last game updates, you can now decorate the interiors and exterior walls of your living houses. Use the hammer and aim at the foundation, the interior walls or the attic. Press the displayed key and the creation menu will open. Depending on the type you can choose different decorations:

> › Wall with window: shutters and curtains
> › Wall with door: various doors and shelves
> › Wall: shelves (inside and outside), candlesticks and trophies
> › Attic: lanterns and himmeli
> › Floor: different carpets

Placing objects

You can place objects from the *building menu* (e.g. tables, chairs, flower pots, lighting) with the *left mouse button* / ⓐ / ⓧ. Note that you can also place plants in flower pots: Aim at the flowerpot, *press E* / ⓐ / ⓧ and select a plant. It has to be in your inventory!

You can also drop any item from your inventory (*X* / ⓧ / ▣ key in inventory). Then aim at the object on the ground and hold down the *E* / ⓐ / ⓧ key. You can now move and drag the item. As soon as you release the *E* / ⓐ / ⓧ key, the item will be dropped.

While you move an object, you can hold down the *left mouse button* / RT / R2 and rotate the object with the *mouse* / ⓡ / ⓡ③ in the desired direction.

This way you can decorate tables, benches, walls, shelves or the floor with clothes, dishes, tools, food and all other things.

If you use food as decoration, make sure you have the *Stop Dropped Items from Spoiling* enabled in the *Gameplay Settings*, otherwise the delicious food on your table will end up being nothing but disgusting garbage the next season! Food will still rot in your inventory and in the chests.

4 Survival

Be quiet for a moment and strain your ears! Listen, can you hear it? It's the howling of the wolves, and let me tell you, they are numerous in the surrounding forest. The people here fear them, sometimes rightly so - but when you think about it, what is the difference between a wolf and a dog if not for the fact that the wolf isn't tamed?

But now that the nights draw out, game and prey becoming scarce, their hunger grows and they become dangerous! Not unlike humans, I tell you! Many a bandit and highwayman would have been an honest and hard working man, if their misery hadn't driven them to do otherwise. In the end, when push comes to shove, we all just want to survive.

And precisely this is not always easy, not in the wilderness surrounding us, nor up here in the North. I remember as an infant often sleeping outside from spring until late autumn having dozed of during the attempt to count all the stars in the night sky. If you try this here, you'll catch your death - well, at least in the colder nights. Hunger, thirst and coldness are your biggest enemies here, you should tremble before them and not before mercenaries or marauders!

More than once, I looked death in the eye, the traumatic fever having worn me out on countless occasions, poisoning having made me reckless and the hastily eaten mushrooms almost snuffing out my life. But the woods give as much as they take and

for he who can read them, who understand them, they offer their gifts more than amply. For every injury or suffering a herb grows - if you believe what the monks say! And I agree with them. Not only that, you can also stave off your hunger, if you search with open eyes. Mushrooms and berries grow plentiful and the right ones keep you well nourished and at strength. Even better is venison or the fish in lakes and rivers, if you know how to catch them.

Cunning and patience are virtues, both for fishing and hunting. It's true that it's easier to get a fish on the hook than it is to kill a deer with a spear or bow – but, which one offers more sustenance?

Obviously the deer my friend, but no human can devour a deer completely by himself. Ah, I already hear you asking if it's not wasteful to kill it? Nay, on no account. Share with others and hope, they will one day show their gratitude. If not, you could learn the skill of preparing food correctly, the knowledge of how to preserve your prey. Then my friend, a slaughtered animal can give you strength for months. And, believe me, there is nothing more scrumptious than smoked ham from a boar! Sadly, I only have the memories of these delicacies left...

What's that, you're asking why?

Look at my gaping mouth and count the remaining teeth! Now you know why there is soup for us today, stew tomorrow, and nourishing porridge with berries and honey the day after tomorrow...

4 Survival

There are many dangers in Medieval Dynasty which could drastically shorten the life of Racimir (or of his son): thirst, hunger, poison, temperatures, wild animals and bandits.

4.1 Eating and Drinking

You have to eat and drink regularly, so that you don't die of thirst or starve. If the food or water bar sinks to 0, you will constantly lose health points.

Beverages

You can drink from every stretch of water, no matter how big it is (stream, pond, river, sea, swamp...). The water's quality is good, no matter the source so you don't have to worry about any poisoning. To carry water, you can use a bucket or a waterskin. Juices nourish you a bit at the same time and alcoholic beverages also decrease poisoning but increase your level of alcohol, which makes you drunk.

> Drink from water sources and from the well.

> Fruits offer some liquid.

> You can fill your bucket or waterskin at any water source and take it with you. The same applies to a bucket of milk, which you can get from breeding animals.

> In your settlement's tavern, you can produce beverages (make juices out of fruits and process them to alcohol).

> You can also buy beverages. However, this is quite unprofitable when it comes to drinking, as you can find water almost everywhere!

Food: for the first days of the game, you have enough food in your inventory.

Collecting: you always find enough mushrooms or berries to eat (except during winter).

Hunting: hunting is more profitable. You get enough meat from traps you set to feed yourself. By hunting, you can quickly acquire enough meat to feed a small village. The bigger the animal, the more meat you get.

Fishing: fishing is another option to acquire food. For the "hunt" for fish you can use any weapon, and the fish do not fight back, like some animals on land.

Farming: you receive fruits, vegetables and cereals. It is more laborious than hunting, but provides many basics for more nourishing and more expensive food (e.g., cereals for flour). Optimally you assign inhabitants to farm instead of doing the hard work yourself.

Animal breeding: regularly provides eggs and milk (depending on the animal). It is also better to employ inhabitants to take care of the animals, to continuously receive food.

Buying: if you don't have the time to look for food, you can buy a variety of meals from vendors. Kitchens and vendors offer prepared food but you can also get raw meat, vegetables and fruits from hunters and farmers.

Medieval Dynasty

Buying Food from Vendors

In the following list, we indicate all the food you can buy from a cook. C/B shows the Cost/Benefit. The smaller the value, the more food you get for your money. For example, per nutritional point, a carrot only costs 0.6 coins whereas a meat pie costs 3.2. BP shows the price you pay at vendors and Bowl indicates if you get a wooden bowl or not. The list is sorted in ascending order by Cost/Benefit (C/B):

Item	BP	Nutrition	Water	Bowl	C/B
Berry	0,3	0,5	1		0.6
Carrot	3	5			0.6
Cabbage	4,5	7			0.6
Beetroot	4,5	6			0.8
Onion	3	4			0.8
Roasted Fish Meat	9	8			1.1
Roasted Meat	7,5	6			1.3
Apple	4,5	3	2		1.5
Fish Meat	6	4			1.5
Cherry	3	2	1		1.5
Plum	3	2	2		1.5
Meat with Gravy	60	30	10	yes	2
Soup	75	35	20	yes	2.1
Dried Fish Meat	15	7			2.1
Porridge	45	20	5	yes	2.3
Gruel	45	20	5	yes	2.3
Pear	4,5	2	3		2.3
Fish	4,5	2			2.3
Stew	60	25	10	yes	2.4
Dried Meat	12	5			2.4

Item	BP	Nutrition	Water	Bowl	C/B
Potage	75	30	10	yes	2.5
Scrambled Eggs	90	35		yes	2.6
Scrambled Eggs with Mushroom	105	40		yes	2.6
Flatbread	120	45			2.7
Salted Fish Meat	27	10	-2		2.7
Wheat Roll	195	67			2.9
Porridge with Apple	90	30	5	yes	3
Vegetable Soup	150	50	25	yes	3
Oat Roll	165	55			3
White Bread	225	60			3
Flatbread with Onions	150	50			3
Egg	15	5			3
Pear Tart	285	85			3.4
Salted meat	24	7	-2		3.4
Wheat Bread	225	65			3.5
Meat Tart	270	75			3.6
Cherry Pie	360	100			3.6
Multigrain Bread	255	70			3.6
Porridge with Berries	75	20	2	yes	3.8
Plum Tart	300	80			3.8
Rye Bread	210	55			3.8
Poppy Seed Pie	345	90			3.8
Meat Pie	330	85			3.9
Fish Tart	270	70			3.9
Fruit Pie	315	80			3.9
Fruit Tart	285	70			4
Mushroom Soup	45	10	20	yes	4.5
Honeycomb	15	2	2		7.5

Cooking

Food has to be cooked before consuming it. You can only eat fruits, vegetables and fish in a raw state without any danger. By eating raw meat, you become poisoned. The additional advantage of cooked food is that it has a higher nutritional value, less weight and you can sell it at a higher price.

» **Campfire**: you can roast meat and fish here.

» **Salting Barrel** in the hunting lodge and the fishing hut: to salt meat and fish.

» **Drying Rack** in the hunting lodge and the fishing hut: to dry meat and fish.

» **Cauldron** in your house and the kitchen: porridges, soups, stews, scrambled eggs, quark and cheese are prepared in the cauldron.

» **Stone Grate** in the kitchen: you can roast meat and fish like you do at campfires. The stone campfire in the houses acts as a stone grate.

» **Stove** in the kitchen: delicious bread, pies, tarts come out of the stove.

» **Juice Press** in the tavern: to produce juice out of fruits.

» **Brewing Station** in the tavern: beer, ale and mead are brewed here.

» **Wine Barrel** in the tavern: you can make wine out of juices.

Food Durabiliy

Over the course of multiple seasons food will spoil. Food laying on the ground spoils instantly at the turn of a season. Milk becomes sour milk, which is used for quark and cheese. In your inventory the durability is short as well (usually 2-3 seasons). It lasts twice as long in a chest. You achieve the longest durability (4x as long as in the inventory) by saving it in the food storage.

List of durability:

Food	Inventory	Chest	Storage time
Vegetables & Fruits	2	4	8
Meat & Fish (fresh and roasted)	2	4	8
Soups, Porridges and Stews	2	4	8
Quark & Cheese	2	4	8
Tarts & Pies	2	4	8
Eggs & Scrambled Eggs	2	4	8
Salted Meat & Salted Fish Meat	3	6	12
Bread	3	6	12
Dried Meat & Dried Fish Meat	4	8	16

The durability of food is reset by further processing it! Grain, herbs and beverages will never spoil.

Seven Year Old Food

Process food at the end of its durability and you will have food for many years: e.g., store meat in the food storage for 8 months and make salted meat out of it, which will last another 12 months. Then, use the salted meat to make stew, which will last 8 months again. Enjoy!

4.2 Poison and Injuries

Injury, Healing, Death

You can lose health points by:

> Being hit by a falling tree

> Falling from a high altitude

> Fighting against animals and bandits

> Poisoning

> Too high or too low temperatures

> Starving or dehydrating

Death

If your health points are reduced to 0, you die. The game and your dynasty ends, unless you have a son, who is at least 18. In this case, you continue the game as the son.

Healing

You can heal by:

> Sleeping in your bed (25 HP)

> Broadleaf Plantain (2 HP)

> Potion of Instant Healing I & II (20/ 50 HP)

> Potion of Healing I & II (60sec/ 1.5 HP per sec & 90 sec/ 2 HP per sec)

Character Stats

These stats influence your character:

Life: see previous page injuries

Stamina: you lose stamina through activities like mining, running or fighting. The tracker mode consumes stamina as well. It regenerates over time and by walking or sleeping. A *Potion of Stamina* reduces the loss of stamina.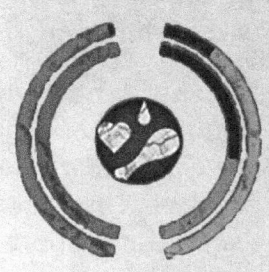

Eating and drinking: see chapter 4.1

Poisoned: you get poisoned by eating rotten food, unripe berries, raw meat; poisonous herbs and mushrooms. You will only take damage once you are 100% poisoned, and food will no longer fill up the food bar. You can heel/lower poisoning with the following remedies:

> › St. John's Wort (-20)

> › Alcoholic beverages (e.g. cherry wine: -5)

> › Potion of Instant Cure (-20)

> › Potion of Cure (60sec/ -2)

Inebriated: by drinking alcoholic beverages or consuming some potions you become drunk (e.g., through the *Potion of Possibilities*, by 100%). When you're drunk, your vision becomes more and more blurred. At 80% and above, you may fall down. This condition decreases over time by itself or you can drink a *Sobriety Potion* (-20 alcohol).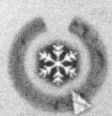

Too cold or **too warm:** you are not wearing the appropriate clothes for the season. Put on some colder or warmer clothes. Campfires warm you up as well. The *Potion of Temperature* lets you tolerate bigger temperature differences for some time.

Dirty: your clothes and you become more and more dirty over time. If you're dirty, mostly the women won't want to speak with you anymore. Take a bath in a *Washtub* filled with water or go into deeper water to clean yourself.

Overburdened: you're carrying too much. Drop something. *Pouches* and *backpacks* increase your carrying capacity as well as the skill *Mule* in the *Extraction* skill tree. The *Potion of Weight* allows you to carry more weight for a short amount of time. Horses and donkeys with saddlebags can carry even more.

Player with pouch on his belt and backpack on his back. The donkey with a large saddlepack maximizes the transport capacity!

4.3   Fights

Wild animals and bandits will get you involved in fights again and again:

> Foxes, lynxes, and badgers only attack you, if you injure them.

> Boars, wolves and wisents act aggressively immediately. From a certain distance, you have a chance to run away as they grunt/howl/bellow in your direction as a warning.

> Bandits always have it in on you. Better you see them before they see you!

Long Distance Fights

Fighting from long distance is always the best option. You're already causing damage while your opponent has to get close to you first before being able to hurt you.

Bows

The advantage of a bow is that you can repeatedly shoot arrows quickly. The drawback is that you consume stamina when drawing the bow. If your stamina sinks to 0, you can't draw the bow anymore!

Name	Damage	Weight	Price
Bow	35	1.25 kg	90
Longbow	55	1.25 kg	230
Recurve Bow	45	1.25 kg	320

Crossbows

Drawing the crossbow is time consuming, but you can aim as long as you want because you don't lose stamina. It does more damage than a bow, but you can't shoot as fast. You have to draw the crossbow every time you equip it!

Name	Damage	Weight	Price
Wooden Crossbow	40	1 kg	150
Iron Crossbow	70	1.25 kg	730

Spear

The spear causes a lot of damage when it's thrown. It also has the advantage that is can be used as a close combat weapon to stab with. Of all the long distance weapons, the spear is the most difficult to aim and hit your target. Unfortunately, it breaks fast, so you should have several in your inventory (carrying capacity!).

Name	Damage	Weight	Price
Wooden Spear	15	1.5 kg	20
Stone Spear	30	2.5 kg	100
Copper Spear	40	2 kg	170
Bronze Spear	50	2 kg	330
Iron Spear	60	2 kg	410

Close Combat Fights

In close combat fights, you are also exposed to the attacks of your opponent.

Spear

The spear is also an excellent close combat weapon, making it a perfect all-rounder. For its values, look at the previous list.

Cudgels

The cudgel is the simplest weapon for a poor farmer. It doesn't have any other use.

Name	Damage	Weight	Price
Cudgel	20	1.5 kg	25
Iron Spiked Cudgel	50	2 kg	180

Knives

Since you always have a knife with you for hunting, it is a good weapon in case your other weapons break.

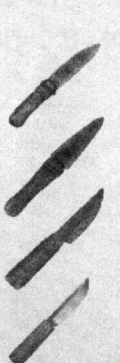

Name	Damage	Weight	Price
Stone Knife	20	0.5 kg	40
Copper Knife	30	0.5 kg	110
Bronze Knife	35	0.75 kg	220
Iron Knife	40	0.75 kg	300

You can also use axes, scythes, sickles, pickaxes, hoes and hammers as a weapon.

Their damage is similar to a knife's, but because you don't hit as fast as with a "normal weapon", you deal less damage. Only use these tools as a last resort, when you don't have anything else to use!

Always Aim for the Head!

Try to always land headshots, because they deal significantly more damage!

Always pay attention to your stamina. If it sinks to 0, you can neither attack nor run away anymore. In any case, most aggressive animals are faster than you, so running away only makes sense before starting a fight with them.

4.4 Experience

For all activities in the game, you gain experience in 2 sectors: in your skills and in your technology level.

Skills

Skills are divided into 6 categories. With *K* / ⊚ / Cⁱ , you open the *Skill Display Screen*. In the picture below, you see the skill tree and above it, you see how much experience you need to progress to the next level of this category:

Extraction

A skill tree that determines how proficient you are in cutting down trees, mining and digging.

➕ 2   ⩔ 3   ⊪ 425.5/750

Depending on your experience, you get skill points which you can use to level up the skills of the corresponding skill tree.

The 6 categories and the activities you need to do to get skill points for them respectively are:

» **Extraction:** felling trees, mining stone, salt and ores from rocks, caves and mines.

» **Hunting:** setting traps, hunting animals with bows, crossbows or spears, skinning animals, crafting items in the hunting lodge.

» **Farming:** working fields and orchards, harvesting fields and orchards, animal breeding, working in the barn (e.g., grinding flour).

» **Diplomacy:** speaking with other people, completing quests, romance and flirting, buying from vendors or selling to them.

» **Survival:** collecting items (stones, sticks, reed, mushrooms, herbs, berries, etc...), fishing.

» **Production:** producing objects of all kind (e.g., in your inventory, in workshops, in the smithies, in sewing huts, in kitchens, in taverns, etc...), salting or drying meat in the hunting lodge.

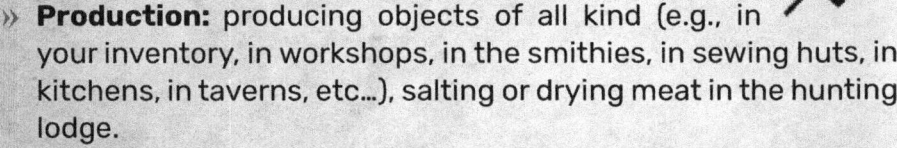

Only the tasks you do yourself give skill points. The activities of your inhabitants don't increase your skill points!

Technologies

The second sector in which you gain experience is technology. There are 4 categories in technology. If you gain enough experience in one of them, you unlock new buildings. Sometimes you can also unlock new *Schemes*, when leveling up a category, which are useful to craft objects. You open the *Technology Display Screen* with *T* / 🎮 / [Cr] .

The 4 technology categories are:

» **Building Technology:** building and repairing buildings, felling trees, mining stones from rocks, caves and mines.

» **Survival Technology:** setting traps, hunting animals, fishing, collecting items (stones, sticks, reed, mushrooms, herbs, berries, etc...).

» **Farming Technology:** creating and working on fields and orchards, harvesting fields and orchards, animal breeding, making items in the barn.

» **Production Technology:** producing objects of all kinds (e.g., in your inventory, in workshops, in smithies, in sewing huts, in kitchens, in taverns, etc...).

> Both you and your inhabitants gather technology experience. So, the activities of your inhabitants also increase the technology experience!

Dynasty Reputation

The dynasty reputation isn't really the same as experience but it reflects your reputation with the inhabitants. The more dynasty reputation you have, the more inhabitants you can invite to your village.

You can display an overview of your reputation, the amount of buildings and of inhabitants you have in the *Management Display Screen* (*N* / ⊚ / Cr).

Your reputation increases by:

» Fulfilling chapter quests (a lot of reputation!).

» Fulfilling quests and challenges.

» Events in which you make honorable and honest choices.

Your reputation decreases by:

» Stealing objects while being seen by somebody. The more valuable the object, the more reputation you lose.

» Killing farm animals.

» Not paying the taxes during spring. The higher your debt, the more you lose reputation.

» Failing quests and challenges.

» Events in which you make dishonest and indecent choices.

If your reputation sinks to -10.000, you are exiled from the valley and the game ends.

4.5 Money

In the game, money is as important as good fighting abilities and a lot of experience.

There is only one currency, the silver coin. Historically, this coin corresponds to the "Pfennig", used in many countries of the Holy Roman Empire or to the English "Penny" or to the French "Denier".

Particularly at the beginning of the game, it is practical to buy many things you can't craft yet or can't get in another way (e.g., seeds and fertiliser for the first sowing or tools and weapons made of metal).

Medieval Dynasty

Expenses

You're confronted with the following expenses in the game:

Annual taxes: during spring, you have to pay the annual taxes. Pay them to Uniegost personally or send your wife to pay them for you. You should have enough money at the end of the year or at least the last day of spring to pay the taxes! Later in the game, the taxes can easily amount to a couple of thousands of coins!

Food: on a journey and no food left? No motivation to hunt or collect? Then buy something to eat from the numerous vendors in the villages. You'll get some food almost everywhere. There's more options in taverns and kitchens.

Raw materials: for your first fields, you have to buy seeds and fertiliser. You can receive a small amount of seeds by completing certain quests but probably not enough. Consider that you receive more seeds after every harvest enabling you to sow more and more seeds each crop cycle. You'll have to buy herbs and mushrooms if the season is not right to collect them. That means that you can save a considerable amount of money by stocking up in the right season! You don't have to buy the other raw materials since you can get them easily enough but if you quickly need some clay and all clay deposits are depleted, you won't care spending money for it.

Tools: you can craft stone tools quickly and easily by yourself but for better tools and weapons made of iron, you will need to fulfill certain requirements. So, why not buy some early in the game? They may be expensive but they are worth it. An iron axe can fell a tree faster and also lasts longer. Shooting iron arrows and bolts make a Robin Hood out of every lame hunter.

Animals: you have to buy your first breeding animals. Just one chicken already costs 1000 coins and a horse costs 10 times more (10.000 coins). Of course, you need 2 animals to breed more of them (hopefully, we don't need to mention that you need one male and one female animal). Smart spenders buy young animals and wait until they become adults. This way, you can save money, but have to wait for them to grow up before they can become productive.

Gifts: you can flirt with women, until one of them accepts your marriage proposal. But you can gain their affection somewhat faster by giving them gifts. Don't forget to give a present to your wife from time to time to ensure her ongoing love. Ask the villagers where you can find the vendor for exotic goods. He always alternates between villages with a tavern (also your village!). A gift costs between 750 and 1500 coins.

Events: events can occur every time the season changes. During some events, you can use coins to prevent a negative effect or to buy an advantage (e.g., during one of the events, you can buy 500 experience points in hunting skill for 1000 coins). Unfortunately, you cannot choose this option if you don't have enough money available!

Waste not, Want not!

You should, if possible, always save up 1500 to 2000 coins, especially before the seasons change. Savings are useful to get the most advantageous outcome of an event or to buy from a vendor when you're in need, sparing you from having to collect money for a long time.

Income

Buying stuff is fun, but how do you actually make money in Medieval Dynasty?

Quests: by fulfilling certain quests and challenges, you are rewarded with coins. Although this is a nice additional income, you'll earn way more money by selling goods in the long run.

Selling: you can sell goods and raw materials you produced in your village or by yourself to vendors. Here are some important basics about selling you should know:

» Every vendor buys your goods for the same price (50% of its value). The ability *Barter* in *Diplomacy* improves the prices.

» You can only sell goods to a vendor as long as he has enough money for it. If you have many goods to sell, you should go to a village with multiple vendors. After the *Changing of the Season*, every vendor will regain his money and his goods.

» At the beginning of the game, *Stone Knives* offer good profits, as they only require a few easy to collect raw materials (2 stones and 5 sticks). They are not that heavy either (=more goods to sell at once) and have a good cost to benefit ratio (20 coins when selling).

» At the beginning of the game, it can also be profitable to steal items and sell them afterwards. Be sure to do this during nighttime and be sure to do your best to remain unseen or you will lose dynasty reputation.

» Later in the game, you should sell the excess goods you have produced. The best is to produce more items with the excess of raw materials, since these can be sold at a better price. If your meat is about to go off, roast it and sell it afterwards!

» Items with a lower durability offer less income: an iron spear with 40% durability means 40% of the retail price. (example: iron spear: 70 coins at 40% instead of 175 coins at 100% durability). This is especially true for food: sell food when it is at 100% of its durability and give food with a low durability to your inhabitants! They don't complain and are happy to have something to eat. (Long live the market economy...)

Market stalls

Later in the game, *Market Stalls* are a good possibility to sell excess goods automatically.

In the *Management Screen* you can assign vendors to stalls and also which wares should be sold.

As soon as you have built a market stall, open the *Management Display Screen*, select a market stall on the building tab and assign a villager to it (*Stallholder*).

Press *C* / Ⓨ / △ to choose the *Type of Goods* sold at the market stall.

1. In the goods trading tab, you can choose the product range, the stallholder should sell.

2. Here, you can see your stock.

3. With *Intensity*, you can fix the amount of wares that should be sold.

4. The bar shows the sales progress of that day.

5. The predicted amount of wares sold within one day.

6. The income per day, if everything goes as planned.

When your storage runs empty, no more products will be sold. Sales will start again automatically as soon as items are available.

Goods Trading – Resources

Icon	Name		Total Skill		Total Work Intensity	
🍞	Stallholder		Diplomacy 1		100%	▼

Assignments

Icon	Name	Status	#	Intensity	Progress	Sale (¼d)	(½d)
🧺	Medium Wicker Basket	Paused	0	◁ 0% ▷	——	0	0
🧺	Wicker Crate	Paused	0	◁ 0% ▷	——	0	0
🧺	Large Wicker Basket	Paused	0	◁ 0% ▷	——	0	0
🧺	Small Wicker Basket	Selling	125	◁ 0% ▷		467	11
🛞	Wooden Wheel	Paused	0	◁ 0% ▷	——	0	0
🥣	Clay Bowl	Paused	56	◁ 0% ▷	——	0	0
🍶	Clay Bottle	Paused	31	◁ 0% ▷	——	0	0
🏺	Clay Jug	Paused	31	◁ 0% ▷	——	0	0
🥛	Clay Cup	Paused	76	◁ 0% ▷	——	0	0

Rye

🪙 2.5   🗄 Resource Storage

A type of crop. Harvested during spring. Can be used for crafting Straw and Rye Grain on the Threshing Floor in the Barn.

5 Hunter & Gatherer

So, you want to know more about hunting? Ha, you're not the only one. We all admire or fear the huntsman, chiefly because he lives solitary in the depths of the forest and rarely comes to the village or tavern. A profession and vocation that makes a man odd, reclusive and sometimes cruel. But not always! I once knew a hunter who was an admirable man and friend, beneath his hard shell and his morose behavior!

But that's nothing you want to hear. Let's talk about hunting then – what's that? You slew an imposing rabbit once? I'm glad to hear it, but that's not hunting, that's trap setting. It's also an art for itself, but a smaller one in my eyes – no offence meant, young friend. What I am talking about is setting out to the forest to face some game, often bigger, heavier and more dangerous than yourself! Well, fine, all in all that's to say only the big deer – and yes, naturally, the bear.

I can remember it very well, me, setting out to the forest to kill a bear. Not because of its flesh, not for using its fur as a clothing – although, it was a nice fur, no, it still is a nice fur. Turn around, behind you it lays, next to my bed and I treat it every weak with flaxseed oil so that it remains shiny. I care about it so much because the bear, which I pulled it over the ears, nearly killed me.

I set out with my good and heavy coat over my shoulders because it was a frosty morning in an even

colder late autumn. The snow had fallen soon, which was not good for the last chores in the fields, but good for me. The bear had left traces in the snow, not only blood drops from the neighbors lamb, but also the big, unmistakable paw prints. I followed them, carrying my bow, with more than a dozen of my best arrows in the quiver and two imposing spears. I followed the beast for hours and finally found it near its cave in which it wanted to retreat. And the fight began! I shot arrow after arrow into its pelt, but it didn't seem to injure it seriously, no, just agitated it, making it furious and enraged! After I shot my last arrow, it ran towards me and I thought my last hour had come. I raised my spear with great difficulty and buried my feet deep into the forests ground. The impact knocked me off my feet, hurled me back a feet against a tree, knocked the air out of my lungs – but, the spear was stuck deep in the bears shoulder.

Injured and roaring, it dragged me to the ground, grabbed me and crushed my body. My rips cracked, its claws pierced my back, and dark clouds began to gather before my eyes. With a last stupendous effort, I fumbled my knife off my belt, the sheath slid to the ground and, repeatedly, with weaker and weaker thrusts, my blade into the monster. It was the fifth stab that pierced its heart and saved my life. Dragging myself to the closest farm nearly drained me of my last strength. The farmer patched me up and helped me to salvage the carcass. What a hunt!

5 Hunter & Gatherer

5.1 The Hunt

Hunting is a good way of obtaining *Meat*, *Leather* and *Pelt*. At the beginning of the game, it is very lucrative, as you can't farm yet. When it comes to hunting, you have three options:

» Hunting with traps

» Go hunting by yourself

» Assign an inhabitant as a hunter in the hunting lodge

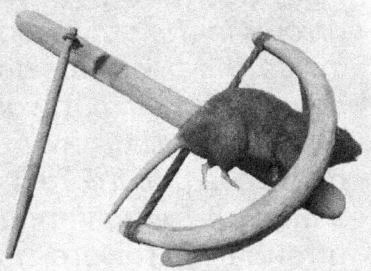

Hunting with Traps

You can craft a *Rabbit Trap* in the building menu. For the other traps, you have to buy the schemes first (50 experience in the *Survival Technology* and 80 coins for the *Bird Trap*; the *Rat Trap* costs 200 coins and 500 experience in *Survival Technology*).

As there are rabbits almost everywhere, it should not be a problem to catch rabbits. Bird and rat traps can also be placed everywhere.

You can place traps anywhere. If there are buildings or the player near a trap, this will have a negative effect on the catching time. At night you can catch animals faster in the traps. The best way to do it is like this: Build traps away from buildings, leave them alone and check what you caught the next morning at the latest! You can set up the used traps again until they break.

Since traps are cheap and can be installed quickly, there are initially an effective method to collect meat, pelt and feathers without much effort. There are not suitable to feed a village with many people.

You can only place one trap of each sort. In the *Hunting Skill Tree*, you can learn the level 3 ability *Trapping Master*. You can level up this ability 3 times. With each gained level you can place more traps, amounting up to 6 traps of each kind. If, later in the game, you don't need traps anymore, you can rearrange your skill points by drinking a *Potion of Possibilities*.

» In addition to meat, *Bird Traps* also provide you with *Feathers,* which you will need later to craft *Arrows*.

» From rabbit traps you get *Meat* and *Pelt*.

Go Hunting

To hunt, you should use a *Bow* with arrows, a *Crossbow* with bolts or a *Spear* you can throw. All other weapons are less suitable, since they can only be used as close combat weapons and most animals flee or attack you, when you're too near to them.

Buy Better Weapons – Now!

By selling stone knives, you can earn enough money at the beginning to buy better weapons. Hunting with a bow and stone arrows is tedious and wooden spears break too fast. However, you can quickly earn the money for a longbow with a few bronze or iron arrows or for 2-3 bronze spears. Hunting is definitely more fun with these and you have the chance to kill most of the animals with one or two headshots! Do it!

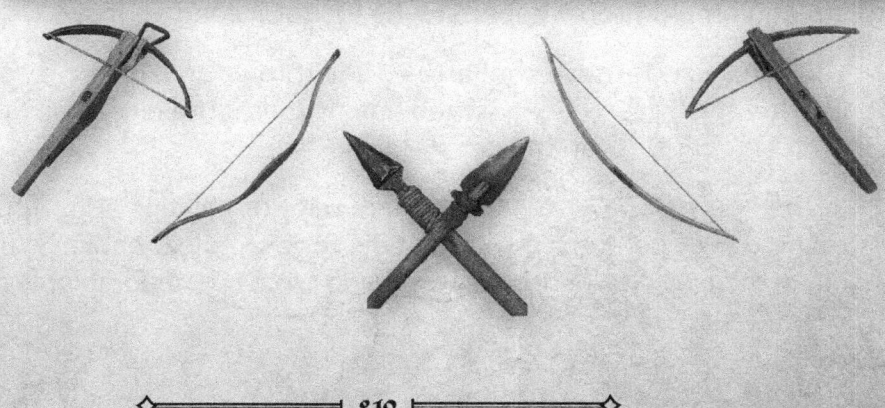

Hunting assistance and tactics

» Many animals make sounds (deers bell, pigs grunt, wolves howl). Follow these sounds to find them quickly.

» Animals always appear in the same area. If you killed or drove away some animals, they will respawn in the same area at a change of the season, unless you block the area by building there.

» Quickly learn the level 2 ability *Tracker* in the *Hunting Skill Tree*. When you press the *Alt* / **LB** / **L1** key, you will be able to see wild animals better (peaceful animals are green and aggressive animals are shown in red).

» A simple hunting formula: stay unnoticed for long + good hunting equipment (iron weapons) + headshot = dead animal

» You can easily retrieve shot arrows and thrown spears by pressing the *Alt* / **LB** / **L1** key, when having learnt the level 2 ability of *Survival Sense* in the *Survival Skill Tree*.

» In the *Hunting Skill Tree*, there are a lot of abilities suited for refining your personal hunting style, for example steadier aiming with bows, faster bow drawing and crossbow loading or less noise while sneaking. Try them out, to see which are best for you! Remember, with a *Potion of Possibilities*, you can rearrange your skill points.

» Some bandits drop a good bow or crossbow with a few arrows on top when you kill them. If you don't want to buy expensive equipment or can't craft it yet, this is a good way to get good hunting equipment!

» The bow shoots fast but aiming consumes stamina. You should use good metal arrows! Buy them, even if they're expensive (or craft them, steal them...)!

» If you hunt with spears, you should always take several of them with you. Hold the *Right Mouse Button* / LT / L2 to get ready to throw and then the *Left Mouse Button* RT / R2 to throw the spear.

» The crossbow doesn't consume stamina while aiming, and is well suited to hunt fast and small animals for which you usually want to aim longer. It's way easier to shoot small animals in the head with a wooden crossbow and good bolts.

» For big and dangerous animals like wisents or bears, 2 head-shots with bronze or iron spears are enough, without having to injure yourself. You only have to be coolheaded enough to stand your ground and throw your second spear, while they storm towards you after the first headshot.

» Many injured animals flee so fast, that you can barely follow them. Follow them anyway if you used *metal weapons* because it makes them blood; blooding animals often die while fleeing. Furthermore, arrows or spears often fall off them while escaping (you can easily find dead animals and your items by pressing the *Alt* / LB / L1 key, provided you have learnt the corresponding ability).

» Fleeing and injured animals stop running after some time and either move normally again or stop to stand still. Follow them at a safe distance, because if you get too close, they will keep on flee-ing.

» If you're a quick and skilled bowman, don't give up on trying to hit a flee-ing and injured animals. One hit is often enough to finish them off.

» Creep up on animals, so that they only notice you late.

» If you slightly miss an animal, it will flee be-cause it noticed the arrow or the spear. If the animal isn't injured, following it is almost never worthwhile. Most of the time, there are going to be other animals of the same kind nearby, which won't be alarmed yet!

» If an arrow is stuck in a dead animal, you can retrieve it but you also get it back by skinning the animal.

Hiring Hunters

If you employ a *Hunter* in the *Hunting Lodge*, he will hunt on his own accord. In the *Buildings Management Menu*, you can decide what the hunter should "produce". If you chose *Meat*, he will go hunting (apart from that, he can salt or dry meat to lengthen its durability).

You see a villager hunting only when there is also huntable game around. The hunter kills peaceful animals such as deer or wild boar. Otherwise he stays in the hunting lodge, but meat is still produced if it is set as production!

For the hunt animation of the fisherman however a fish is spawned extra. The fisherman "produces" fish fillet instead of meat.

On the following pages, you have an overview of all the wild animals and where to find them in the valley.

Apart from their behavior, you also learn about the animal's pack size, their loot and can read a brief description with hunting tips.

Online Interactive Map

On our online map of Medieval Dynasty, you can view all the spots where you can find game (and even more!). You find the interactive map on:

www.bildner-verlag.de/en/medieval-dynasty

You can also buy these pieces of information from the hunters of the valley: *Hunter Gizela* in *Lesnica* and *Hunter Raymund* in *Tutki*:

Talk to the hunter and ask *Where can I find...* and select *Wild Animals*. Then, she marks the spots of the respective animal on your map for the price of 500 to 5000 coins. The spots also automatically appear when you walk past them.

Open the *Map* (M / ◉ / Crl) and switch to *Wild Animals* with the *Filters* arrows / ◆◆ ◆◆ / ◆◐ ◐◆. You can't apply further filters. So, if you bought or found the spawning spots of all animals, you have to take a closer look at the map:

Animal	Price
Rabbit	500
Badger	1000
Moose	2000
Boar	2000
Wisent	4000

Animal	Price
Fox	750
Deer	1000
Lynx	1500
Wolf	3000
Bear	5000

Animal	Price
Pigeon	250
Duck	250
Crow	500
Hawk	1000
White-tailed Eagle	1500

Bear

Behavior	Aggressive
Danger:	High
Amount:	1-2
Loot from skinning:	
Meat	25
Leather	10

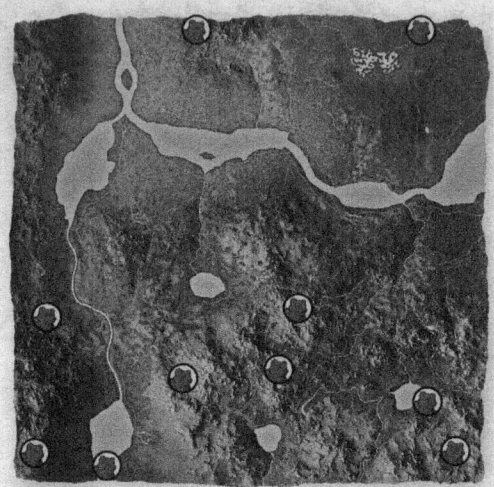

Description:

Bears are mostly found in the mountains, near caves (luckily not IN caves). Stay away from them, because in close combat they can injure you badly.

When hunting them, creep up on them and try to shoot them in the head twice from a secure distance. With a bit of luck, this will be enough. In close combat, a bear will rear up now and again to aim a blow at you with its paws. Use this opportunity to move away and shoot at it with an arrow or throw a spear.

Bears flee, as soon as they are badly injured. Follow them, because they often die with one last hit or even during their flight!

Badger

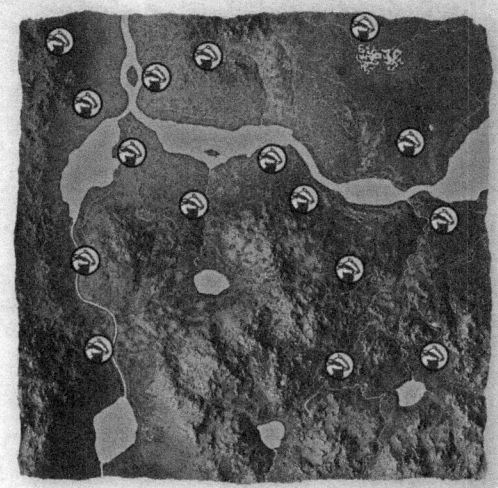

Behavior:	Passive
Danger:	Low
Amount:	2-3

Loot from skinning:

Meat	4
Fur	3

Description:

Badgers flee, as soon as they notice you but they will retaliate if you attack them. They are small and very fast, so they are not easy to hit. Nevertheless, 1-2 blows with a good metal weapon can kill them.

Badgers, foxes and lynxes behave very similarly. If you have found yourself a good hunting tactic for one of these animals, it will also work for the others.

If they flee, following them is not worthwhile. Creep up on them, wait until the
animal is in a good position and
kill it with a single headshot. To do this, a crossbow is very helpful as
you can aim with it
continually.

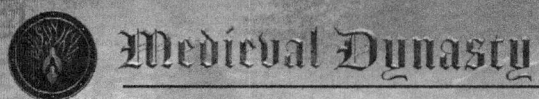

Medieval Dynasty

 Moose

Behavior:	Flight
Danger:	None
Amount:	2-4
Loot from skinning:	
Meat	20-22
Leather	5
Chance to get a skull	

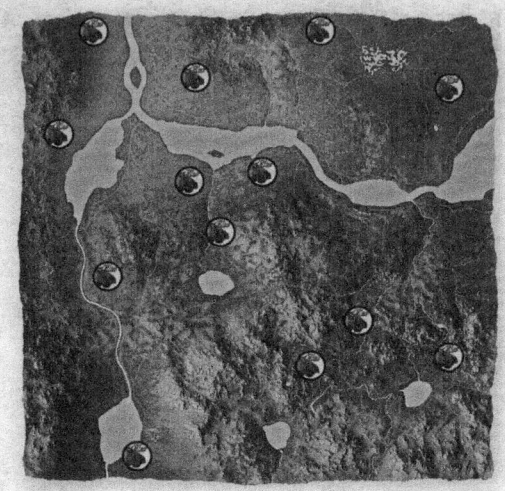

Description:

In the game, moose are actually just like bigger deers. You often find a male moose together with two to three female moose. They flee, as soon as they notice you or are injured. They run very quickly, so catching up with them is almost impossible.

Sneak up on them and try to kill them instantly with a headshot. Since they have more health points than a deer, this doesn't always work, though.

Instead of pursuing them, wait for a short time and then search the area within a bigger radius (*Alt* / LB / L1 key!). Badly wounded animals often die during their flight.

 Fox

Behavior:	Passive
Danger:	Low
Amount:	2-3

Loot from skinning:

Meat	6
Fur	2

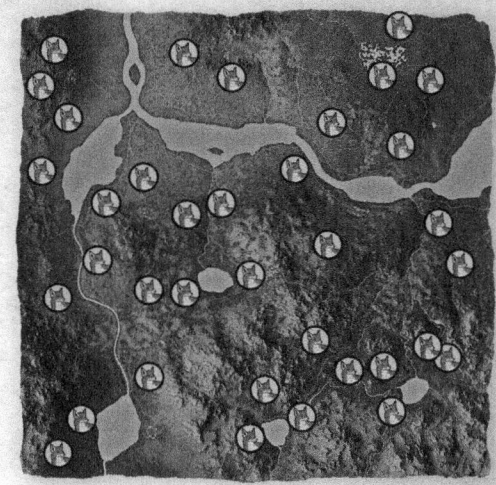

Description:

The fox only attacks you, if you injure it first. If not, it immediately flees. You can even kill it with less efficient weapons. You only have to land 1-2 hits with metal weapons.

In close combat, it shouldn't pose much of a threat, unless you're already badly injured and don't possess good weapons, in which case it would be unwise to attack in the first place.

 **Rabbit**

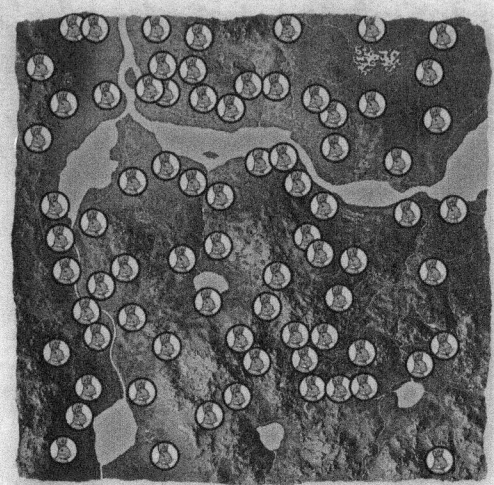

Behavior:	Flight
Danger:	ENORMOUS :)
Amount:	1-4
Loot from skinning:	
Meat	2
Fur	2

Description:

Rabbits are found almost everywhere. They flee, as soon as you approach them. They are not easy to hunt, mainly because they never hold still.

It's better to place rabbit traps in a rabbit area and to come back after a while to collect the loot.

Rabbits are perfect to practice your aim, as they are small and fast. If you can hit a lolloping rabbit with your bow, it should be easy to hit an assailing wisent in the head.

You gain very little from a rabbit though, making it only useful to feed yourself.

 **Deer**

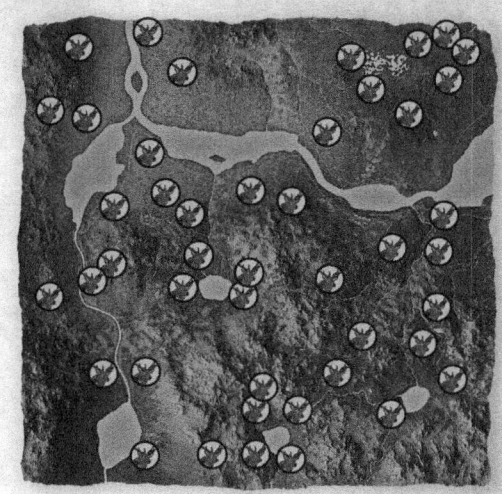

Behavior:	Flight
Danger:	none
Amount:	3-4

Loot from skinning:

Meat	15-18
Leather	3
Chance to get a skull	

Description:

You'll always come across deers in small herds. Most of the time, you find one stag along with 2-3 does. As soon as they notice you, the deer flee. They are very fast even when shot, making catching up with them quite diffi-cult.

As always, the best method is to land a single headshot, killing it instantly, preferably with an iron weapon or a good bow. In comparison, hunting deers with wooden spears is very laborious and could almost be called masochistic.

You can notice deers from far away by their loud grunts.

 **Lynx**

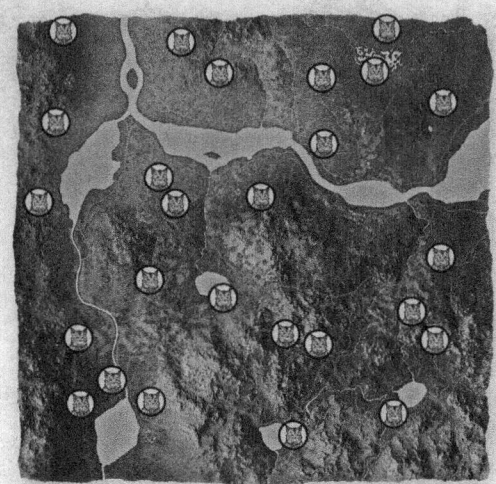

Behavior:	Passive
Danger:	Low
Amount:	1-2

Loot from skinning:

Meat	8
Fur	2

Description:

Like the badger and the fox, the lynx flees as soon as it notices you. It only attacks, if you injure it first. It is an easy to kill opponent. With good equipment (metal weapons), you can dispose of it quickly and easily.

The best method to hunt lynxes is to sneak up on them. Use the *Alt* / LB / L1 key to see where they are. With a good bow and metal arrows, you can kill a lynx with a single headshot.

Another method is to injure it with an arrow first and to wait for it to attack you in close combat. Now, you can kill it with a close combat weapon.

 **Boar**

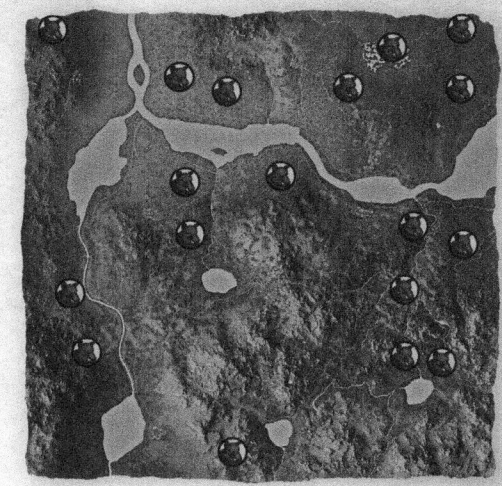

Behavior:	Aggressive
Danger:	Normal
Amount:	2-3
Loot from skinning:	
Meat	8
Leather	3

Description:

Whether in real life or in the game, boars are dangerous animals and not to be underestimated. Some real life noblemen lost their lives while hunting boars during medieval times. If you're too close, they will attack you immediately. If they notice you from a further distance, they stop and grunt in your direction.

That's the best moment to headshot them (arrow or spear). Metal weapons only require a single shot.

When there's more than one boar or if you're already injured, close combat becomes quite the challenge. Be careful!

Wisent

Behavior:	Aggressive
Danger:	High
Amount:	2-4
Loot from skinning:	
Meat	25
Leather	7
Chance to get a skull	

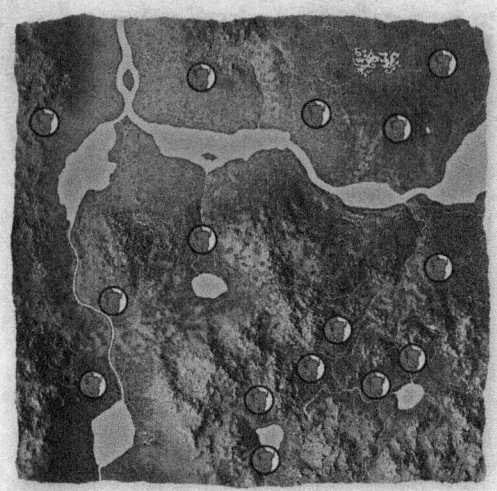

Description:

The wisent is a European bison and nearly extinct nowadays (thanks to breeding, in the whole world there are approx. 3000 wisents remaining worldwide). In the game, it is one of the most dangerous animals, as it is fast, strong and aggressive. Wisents are nearly always roaming around in groups of 3. If you're not specifically out to hunt them, you should avoid them at a great distance. If they attack you, you should injure them as fast as possible, to make them flee. Escaping from them is almost impossible.

Headshots are very important when hunting wisents, as they have many health points. Two well placed headshots with iron spears are enough to kill a wisent.

 ## Wolf

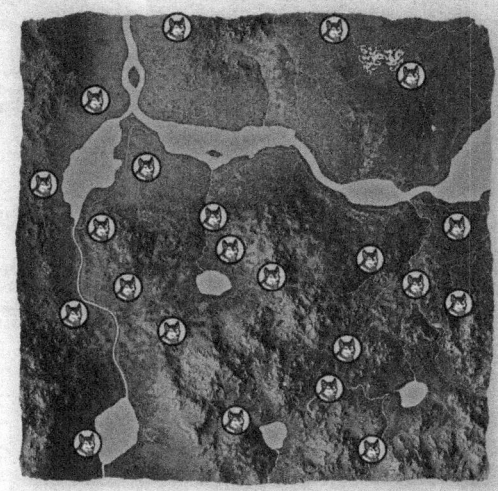

Behavior::	Aggressive
Danger:	Normal
Amount:	2-4
Loot from skinning:	
Meat	12
Fur	3

Description:

Wolves are often in packs of three. If a wolf notices prey (e.g., a rabbit or a deer), it will hunt it. If you notice a wolf early enough, you can easily escape or kill it. If it sees you, it pauses for a moment, lift its head and howl as a warning. This is when you can run away or headshot it.

If you get too close to a wolf, it attacks you immediately. Nearby wolves are a further threat. If you get into close combat, you should hit its head several times, to make it flee. If you have good equipment (metal spear) and are at full health, close combat with a wolf should not be a problem.

Birds

You can encounter five different bird species in the world of Medieval Dynasty. They can all be hunted and reward you with different prey. We have listed the exact data here in a table:

Bird	Loot from Skinning
White-tailed Eagle	6 Meat, 30 Feather
Hawk	5 Meat, 24 Feather
Duck	4 Meat, 10 Feather
Dove	2 Meat, 10 Feather
Crow	4 Meat, 16 Feather

White-tailed Eagle

Crow

Duck

Hawk

Pigeon

5.2 Fish

In order to fish, you need a *Fishing spear*. Go into a stretch of water and look for fish. On the following map, you can see all the places, where you can find some. Throw the fishing spear or use it to stab. If you hit a fish, it's instantly placed into your inventory. If thrown, the spear must be retrieved, hopefully with a fish on it! You can also use other weapons (and even catch them with your hands!).

You can fish for 3 types of fish:

	Roach	1 fish meat
	Perch	4 fish meat
	Pike	7 fish meat

You can roast the fish over a campfire or make fish meat in the fishing hut, the latter of which is more effective. You can ask the fisher *Bytomir* in *Jezerica* to mark the locations of all three types of fish on your map.

Assigned Fishers

A fisher catches fish spawned especially for him during his fishing. Any existing fish is not removed. A fisher only "produces" fish meat and doesn't really fish any of the 3 types listed above. Only you can fish these! In addition, you can salt or dry meat and fish in the fishing hut.

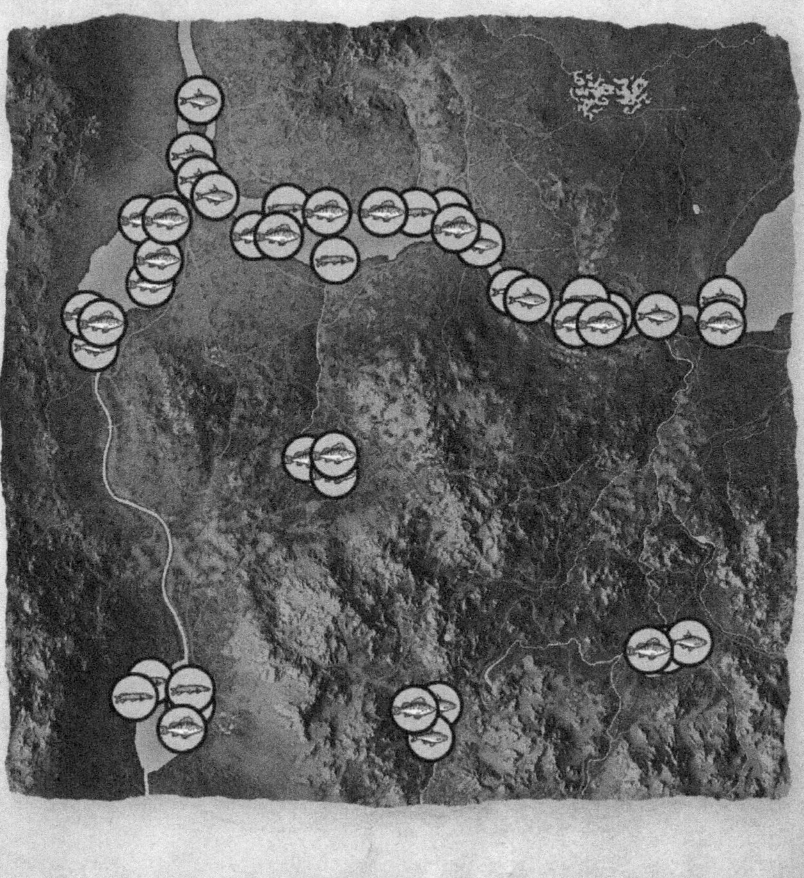

Medieval Dynasty

Fishing Nets

Just like setting traps whilst hunting you can also set fish traps in waters – fishing nets.

They exist in small, medium and big sizes:

Size	Caught Fishes	Building Price	Scheme Price
Small	3-4 Roaches	2 sticks 6 linen threads	250
Medium	3-4 Perches	2 sticks 9 linen threads	750
Big	3 Pikes	2 sticks 12 linen threads	1500

By default you can build one net of each size. You have to place the nets inside water, no matter if in lakes, ponds, rivers or creeks.

With the ability *Trapping Master* of the *Hunting Skill Tree*, the amount of traps you can set increases.

Depending on the level of the ability, you can build 2, 4 or 6 traps of each size!

If you set 6 nets of each size in any water, you will receive up to 54 fish, which almost corresponds to 600 fish meat!

You can use each net up to 3 times, after that it will be destroyed and you have to build a new one!

Fishing or Hunting?

Regardless if you yourself or one of your villagers is doing it, hunting is more effective than fishing. You get more meat than fish meat and also further resources. However, fishing with many nets can be very lucrative and doesn't put you at risk!!

5.3 Mushrooms, Herbs & Tinctures

Searching & Collecting

By now, you probably know how to collect mushrooms, berries and herbs. The level 2 ability *Survival Sense* of the *Survival Skill Tree* helps with that by highlighting mushrooms, berries and herbs when pressing *Alt* / **LB** / **L1** to activate the inspector mode.

You can find mushrooms, berries and herbs almost everywhere, making us indicating their location unnecessary. By walking around every season, you find all you need!

You can eat most herbs on the spot, but their effects are quite minor (feeding or healing). However, you can brew many effective potions from them in the herbalist's hut.

Be careful, mushrooms and some herbs are poisonous to eat (see table on the right) !

The list details which herbs can be found during which season:

Name	Spring	Summer	Autumn	Winter
Unripe Berries (poisonous 20%) ☠	X	-	-	-
Ripe Berries	-	X	-	-
St. John's Wort	X	X	X	-
Broadleaf Plantain	X	X	X	-
Daisy	X	X	-	-
Dandelion	X	X	-	-
Chicory	X	X	X	-
Thistle	-	X	-	-
Henbane (poisonous 2%) ☠	-	X	-	-
Deadly Nightshade (poisonous 50%) ☠	-	X	-	-
Morel Mushroom (poisonous 0.5%) ☠	X	-	-	-
Red Pine Mushroom (poisonous 0.5%) ☠	-	-	X	-
Wolly Milkcap Mushroom ☠ (poisonous 50%)	-	-	X	-
Bolete Mushroom (poisonous 0.5%)	-	-	X	-
Bitter Bolete Mushroom (poisonous 50%) ☠	-	-	X	-
Parasol Mushroom (poisonous 0.5%) ☠	-	-	X	-
Fly Agaric Mushroom (poisonous 100%) ☠	-	-	X	-

Making Potions

In the herbalist's hut, you can produce various potions. Healing potions, potions of night vision, potions enabling you to rearrange all your skills abilities, and many more can be made by yourself or by your inhabitants.

Villagers employed in the hut

A worker in the herbalist's hut can both collect ingredients and make potions. Just like with all other workers, you can determine what he should do in the *Management Display Screen* (*N* / ◎ / ⌨). Open the hut on the left side of the screen and on the right side, choose what the villager should collect and produce by selecting *Goods Production*.

A villager can only collect ingredients available in the current season. To ensure he collects, you have to adapt his tasks at every season change!

Production of potions

To make a potion, you must already possess the corresponding scheme! You can find the schemes in *Survival Technology* under the herbalist's hut I and II.

For a potion you always need:

> A wooden or a clay vial

> Herbs or mushrooms

> A bucket of water

You can produce *vials* in a workshop, as soon as you have bought the schemes. You can also buy vials from *Falibor* in *Borowo*.

You can get a bucket of water from the well, fill one by yourself at any water source or buy one from vendors (e.g., from the *Animal Breeder* in *Gostovia*).

Some potions require *Hop*, *Poppy Seeds* or *Mead* as an additional ingredient.

Tips for potions:

> You should always carry 1-2 healing potions with you.

> The potion of night vision only helps you to see better in caves, if you additionally use a torch. It does not help in absolute darkness, since you always need some remaining light (stars, torch...). (Think of it as an amplifier of remaining light!).

> The potion of weight briefly helps you to carry more. For long distances, you will need many potions.

Potion List

All the potions you can make at the workbench in the herbalist's hut, are listed below. Scheme & value stands for the price of a scheme and the value of the potion.

Name	Effect	Ingredients	Scheme & Value
Potion of Instant Healing I	+20 health instantly	Wooden Vial 1x Broadleaf Plantain 2x Dandelion 2x Bucket of Water 1x	250 40
Potion of Instant Healing II	+50 health instantly	Clay Vial 1x Broadleaf Plantain 4x Dandelion w4x Bucket of Water 1x	550 50
Potion of Healing I	+1,5/s for 60 sec health (=90 health)	Wooden Vial 1x Broadleaf Plantain 5x Dandelion 5x Bucket of Water 1x	250 40
Potion of Healing II	+2/s for 90 sec health (=180 health)	Clay Vial 1x Broadleaf Plantain 10x Dandelion 10x Bucket of Water 1x	550 50
Potion of Instant Cure	-20% poisoning	Wooden Vial 1x St. John's Wort 2x Thistle3x Chicory 3x Bucket of Water 1x	250 40

Name	Effect	Ingredients	Scheme & Value
Potion of Cure	-2%/s for 60 sec poisoning (-120 poisoning)	Clay Vial 1x St: John's Wort 2x Dandelion 4x Henbane 4x Bucket of Water 1x	550 50
Potion of Sobriety	-20 % alcohol	Clay Vial1x Daisy 2x Thistle 2x Bucket of Water 1x	550 50
Potion of Health	+50 more health for 120 sec	Clay Vial 1x Broadleaf Plantain 5x Dandelion 5x Daisy 5x Poppy Seed 2x Bucket of Water 1x	550 60
Potion of Stamina	50% less stamina consumption for 120 sec	Wooden Vial 1x Chicory 5x Dandelion 5x Bucket of Water 1x	250 40
Potion of Satiety	50% less food consumption for 120 sec	Clay Vial 1x Chicory 5x Hop 1x Bucket of Water 1x	550 50
Potion of Saturation	50% less water consumption for 120 sec	Wooden Vial 1x Daisy 4x Hop 1x Bucket of Water 1x	250 40
Potion of Weight	+20 kg weight limit for 240sec	Wooden Vial 1x Poppy seed 5x Henbane 5x Bucket of Water 1x	250 60

Medieval Dynasty

Name	Effect	Ingredients	Scheme & Value
Potion of Temperature	+4 Temperature tolerance for 240 sec	Woden Vial 1x Hop 5x Bucket of Water 1x	250 50
Potion of Strength	+50% more damage for 120 sec	Wooden Vial 1x Henbane 5x Bucket of Water 1x	250 40
Potion of Night Vision	Night vision for 120 sec	Clay Vial 1x Deadly Nightshade 10x Henbane 5x Bucket of Water 1x	550 50
Poison	100% poisoning ingredient for poisoned arrows & poisoned bolts	Wooden Vial 1x Deadly Nightshade 5x Bucket of Water 1x	250 40
Potion of Camouflage	Better camouflage for 60 sec	Clay Vial 1x Bolete Mushroom 3x Parasol Mushroom 3x Red Pine Mushroom 3x Morel Mushroom 3x Bucket of Water 1x	550 80
Potion of Possibilities	+ 100% alcohol resets all the skills to rearrange your abilities	Clay Vial 1x Bitter Bolete Mushroom 5x Fly Agaric Mushroom 5x Woodly Milkcap Mushroom 5x Mead 1x	550 80

Poisoned arrows and bolts

At the workbench, you can make *Poisoned Arrows* for bows and *Poisoned Bolts* for crossbows. If you hit an animal with one of these, it can poison the animal and cause more damage over time! You need 10 arrows or bolts of one type (e.g., 10 copper arrows) and a poison vial. The better the quality the arrow/bolt has, the more the animal is poisoned.

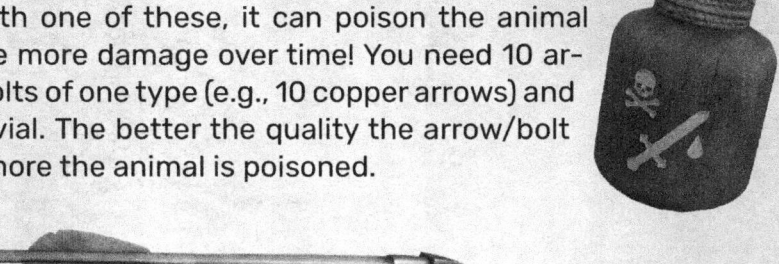

Benefits of poisoned arrows:

› A poisoned arrow assures that you kill your target, even if it escapes.

› You can hit animals like bears and wisents from a secure distance and then flee, before they get to you. If you aimed well, the animal should die while following you!

› The same tactics can be used for bandits, who haven't noticed you.

6 Farming & Animal Breeding

'm pleased to hear you're at least thinking about staying here with us. It's not an easy life, but you can achieve a lot with hard work, courage and two capable hands – look at me! When I staggered over that hill behind us, I didn't possess a lot more than the clothes on my back, some supplies and a few copper coins. But today, my sons, my grandchildren and my nephews nearly possess every third house here.

How did I managed this, you may ask? Well, the most honest and reliable way to prosperity is still made of land and meadow, fields and vegetable gardens. A trade in hand finds gold in every land but dynasties are built on farms.

He who harvests his own grains, can bake bread without buying flour. Just as harvesting your own beetroots will save you from famine during winters. He who has many animals in his stables, is respect-ed and will be asked for advice. You see what I'm try-ing to say. A flock of chickens is good to begin with, the eggs provide you with supplementary earnings and an with a highly delicious ingredient for lus-cious meals. He who possess sheep and lambs can easily earn coin with the wool and pigs...

Ha, pigs! Did you hear the Tale of old Pjotr? No? He lives in the small valley in the South-East, all alone in a farm, he built himself. Well, not all by himself. It probably was four or five winters ago, his son moved to Prague and married, his daughters likewise moved out a long time ago and he has been a widower for many years now. The harvest had been gathered in, the cellar full of beetroots and a single sow was left in the pigsty – waiting for spring, to be inseminated and give birth to a new litter of piglets. Poor Pjotr was mending the roof, as he fell unluckily and broke his leg multiple times – ha, not a pleasant sight!

He couldn't move, was barely able to drag himself into his house – but there was no one there who could have helped him anyway. He roared for aid until he became hoarse and his screams died away without anyone hearing them.

The next day, the sow became agitated, because it hadn't been fed and made its way to the cellar. First, it feasted on the beetroots before getting curious and going into the house, where Pjotr was laying more dead than alive. And the sow...

... No, the sow didn't eat him, that's what I would also have expected! Instead, it grabbed her master by his boots with its snout and dragged him all the way to the next village. Pjotr's clothes were torn to shreds, his back badly covered in scratches – but he survived, with a stiff leg, but he survived. He still endures, even tough he has to pay one of the young lads from the village by now, to take over the hard work and long journeys.

What's that? Ah, the sow? Yes, it is still alive, but does not live in the pigsty any more, no! It now shares the house with Pjotr, more dog than pig, even sleeps next to his bed. Perhaps sometimes even in it, who knows? But one thing is certain, old Pjotr has not eaten a bite of pork since that day.

6 Farming & Animal Breeding

6.1 Work the Fields

Farming is a reliable way of providing you with enough food and raw material (straw), but it requires some effort:

From the start of the game you can cultivate fields. You don't necessarily need a barn to do so.

If you want a villager to cultivate the fields in your place, you first have to build a **Barn** and employ him there as a **Farmer**.

Sowing and harvesting are only possible during a specific season, depending on the respective plants. You can't cultivate a plant in the wrong season.

Harvested vegetables can be used without processing (e.g., eat or cook it). Grain needs to be threshed first in order to receive straw and grains. You can only do that at the **Crafting Stations** of **Barns**! There you can also process the grain into flour.

Needed Resources and Tools

You need the following things to cultivate the fields by yourself:

	Hoe	To plough the fields after their creation and fertilisation.
	Simple bag	To spread out fertiliser and seeds on the fields.
	Bag	The more durable alternative of the simple bag.
	Fertiliser	Before sowing, you have to spread fertiliser over the fields and then plough them with the hoe.
	Seeds	Seeds of the respective crops. Sow them with a simple bag or a bag.
	Seedling	A very young tree for an orchard.
	Sickle	To harvest cereals.
	Scythe	The bigger and more effective alternative to the sickle.

Farmers employed in your barn need these resources in the *Resource Storage* or in the *Chest* of the *Barn* to work properly.

When you're just starting out you have to buy your first *Seeds* or you can eventually get some as quest rewards. From the harvest, you collect enough seeds to sow again.

You can make *Fertiliser* yourself at the *Workbench* of a *Barn* out of rotten food (*Rot*) or of *Manure* from pigs (animal husbandry) and *Straw*.

Creating Fields

To cultivate fields, follow the explanations below (provided that you already have the needed resources and the tools in your inventory):

» Open the creation menu (*Q* / RB / R1) and select Building – Farming – Field.

» You see a green post. Place it on an unoccupied area. That is the first corner of your field. Now, move diagonally in the direction you want your field to be. You should now see several land parcels appearing. The amount of parcels is displayed in the bottom center of the screen (e.g., 4x5 means 4 parcels high, 5 parcels wide = 20 parcels in total for this field).

» If the area is shown red, something is blocking the building site (e.g., a tree, a road or uneven terrain).

» Then, you have to grub each parcel separately with a *Hoe*. You only have to do this when creating a new field.

» Use the (*Simple*) *Bag* and select the *Fertiliser* with the *Right Mouse Button* / LT / L2 . Then, spread the fertiliser on the grubbed up (or later harvested) parcels by using the *Left Mouse Button* / RT / R2 .

» Now, you have to plough the parcels with the *Hoe* again.

» Now, use the (*Simple*) *Bag* again and select the seeds you want with the *Right Mouse Button* / LT / L2 . With the *Left Mouse Button* / RT / R2 , you sow the *Seeds* on a parcel.

From left to right: grubbed, fertilized, ploughed, sowed

» Now, you have to wait for the harvesting season.

» You can harvest ripe vegetables (like cabbage or carrots) with your hands. For cereals, you need a scythe or a sickle.

» After that, you have to fertilise the field again, plough it with the hoe and sow seeds again.

Workers in the barn

There are two types of workers with completely different tasks in the *Barn*:

Farmers: work your fields, grub them, fertilise them, plough them, sow seeds and harvest (can only grub and harvest orchards).

Barn Workers: they produce goods made from the harvest of the fields: they thresh *Cereals* into *Grains* and *Straw*, grind grains into *Flour* and produce *Fertiliser*.

In the *Management Screen Display* under *Buildings*, you can assign any inhabitant to the barn and in the *Goods Production* window, you can decide which products the barn workers should produce.

On the following page, you find the different stages of farming: sowing, growing and harvesting. The wheat has been sowed during spring, has grown green during summer and is ready for harvesting in autumn:

Field Management

In the *Management* menu, you can decide what your farmers sow on your fields.

» Open the menu with *N/⊚/⌘* and on the top left choose fields **1**.

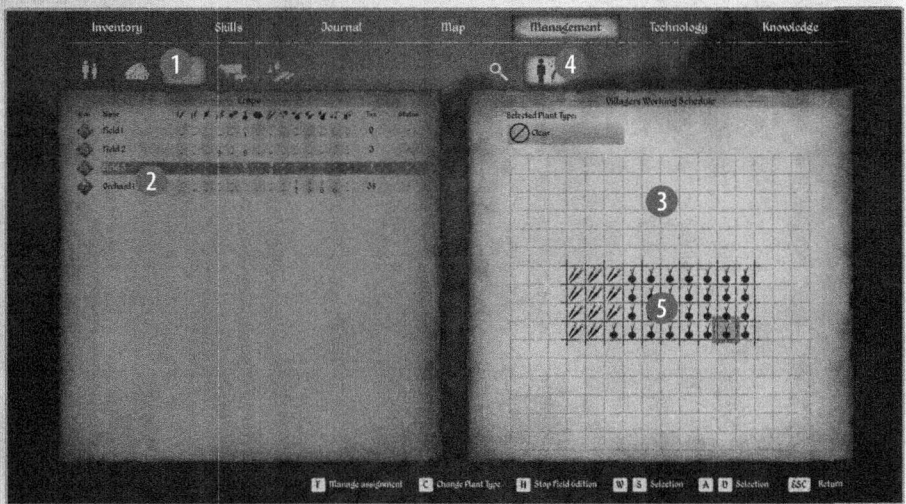

» *Double-Click /⬨/⊗* to open a field **2**. Here you can also give a field its own name.

» On the right side, you can see how big the field is **3** and what its current status is.

» Change to the working schedule view **4** at the top right and press *C /Ⓨ/⬨* to select the new crops to be cultivated here. (Don't forget, that there should be enough seeds and fertiliser in the resource storage or in the chest of the barn!)

» Select the crops on the left side and mark the parcels where the vegetable should be cultivated on the right side **5**. You can cultivate different plants on the same field!

Micromanagement

» A single worker can till an approx. 40x50 big field in one season (fertilizing, ploughing and sowing).

» Just as important is the distance between the residential houses, the barn and the fields. These distances should be as small as possible, because farmers don't work while on the way!

» If there is much to do, you can also temporarily employ other villagers as farmers. Of course, you can also assist your farmers yourself, if they won't be able to finish their jobs during a season. The first times they cultivate fields, watch if they can manage all fields or if some of the parcels remain untouched! Unharvested crops are lost at the change of season!

» You can make villagers alternately work as farmers and barn workers: during spring as a farmer to sow grains. During summer, the crops are growing and the farmer has nothing to do. Reassign him as a barn worker to produce fertiliser, grains and flour. During autumn, you change him back to a farmer for the harvest. In winter, there is no work on the fields, you can assign him as a barn worker again.

Medieval Dynasty

Orchards

Orchards (*Hops* also count as fruit in the game) function like the fields but much easier:

» You (or a farmer) have to create an orchard like a field in the creation menu (*Q* / RB / R1).

» You have to grub the orchard with the *Hoe*.

» No additional ploughing or fertilizing needed.

» You sow the *Seedlings* with a (*Simple*) *Bag* (select with the *Right Mouse Button* / LT / L2 and sow with the *Left Mouse Button* / RT / R2).

» After about 3 seasons, the seedlings will have grown to the point where they bear fruit for the first time. They will be fully grown only after about 3 years. They will bear more fruit each year until they are fully grown. Each summer you can plow the ripe fruit with your bare hand or have a farmer do this work for you. Hops are ready for harvest in the fall.

During spring, the orchards blossom. You can see the hops on the left side.

Sowing & Harvesting

Grain	Sowing	Harvest
Wheat	Spring Autumn	Autumn Summer
Oat	Spring	Autumn
Rye	Autumn	Spring
Flax	Spring	Summer
Carrot	Spring Winter	Autumn Summer
Cabbage	Spring Summer	Summer Autumn
Beetroot	Spring	Autumn
Onions	Spring	Summer
Poppy	Spring	Autumn

» It doesn't matter when you plant orchards or hops. They need 3 seasons to grow. In the following year, you will be able to pick the fruits in summer or autumn. You won't have to replant them after the harvest.

6.2 Animal Husbandry

As soon as you have enough experience in farming technology, you can build stables and begin with animal husbandry.

» First, build the respective *stable* for the animal you want (see the list of animals on the following pages). Without the corresponding stable, you can't buy any animals.

» Go to the village with the corresponding *Animal Breeder* (again see the following list of animals). You don't buy animals directly from vendors (sometimes there isn't even a NPC), instead, you just go into the stable and select the animal to buy it. The price is displayed on the screen. The animal will move to your stable on its own.

» If you didn't assign a villager to the stable, you have to put animal feed in the feeding trough by yourself. You need some in your inventory to do this. Then hold the indicated key while looking at the trough or at the feeding rack and it's filled with food.

» You can buy animal feed from animal breeder or make it in the barn from straw, rye grain and oat grain.

» As soon as you have one male and at least one female animal, they will reproduce automatically until the stable is full.

» You can kill your animals anytime and then skin them, to get leather or feather depending on the animal. However, this is rather unprofitable.

» Animal products like eggs and manure can be collected by animal breeders or by yourself. You can choose what they should produce in the *Management display screen*.

» Animals can be marked for sale in the *Management display screen*. The animals will be immediately sold (press and hold *X* / ⊗ / ◻).

» During the day, the animals wander around their stable and go back inside it at night. Don't worry, the animals won't escape, even if they sometimes make it to the other end of your village! You can confine them with a closed fence. Gates provide openings that keep animals out but let workers through.

Farming or Animal Husbandry?

When it comes to food and resource production, animal husbandry is far less productive than a large scale crop production. However, you receive some raw materials (e.g., eggs, wool, bucket of milk, manure) from animal husbandry, which you could otherwise only buy.

Medieval Dynasty

 Chicken

Buy in:	Borowo Rolnica
Male animal:	1125
Female animal:	1125
Young male animal:	563
Young female animal:	563
XP in farming:	100
Average life span	6.25y

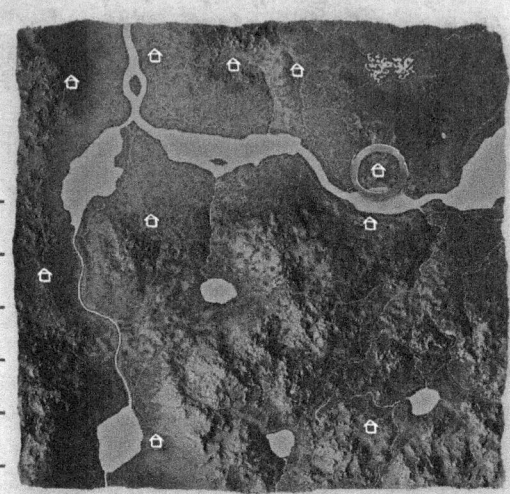

Description:

With a villager as an animal breeder in the *Henhouse*, you produce mainly *Eggs* but also feathers . Chickens reproduce relatively fast and they are also grow up quickly. If you want to save money, buy young animals (chicks). You can also get eggs and feathers from the nests yourself.

If at some point you have too many chicken (or roosters!), you can slaughter them to receive 10-15 feathers and 4 meat or sell them. Female animals offer less resources on average. Young animals provide approx. half the resources.

Goose

Buy in:	Gostovia
Male animal:	1500
Female animal:	1500
Young male animal:	750
Young female animal:	750
XP in farming:	500
Average life span:	12,5y

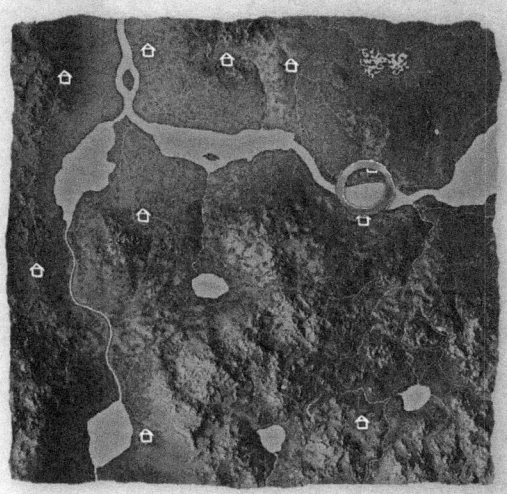

Description:

Geese are housed in the *Goose House* and, in contrary to the chickens, produce more *Feathers* and less eggs, which you can also get by yourself from the nests. Geese do not reproduce as quickly as chickens, but have a longer life expectancy.

By slaughtering a goose, you get 8 meat and 12-17 feathers.

Medieval Dynasty

Goat

Buy in:	Denica
Male animal:	3000
Female animal:	3000
Young male animal:	1500
Young female animal:	1500
XP in farming:	2500
Average life span	15y

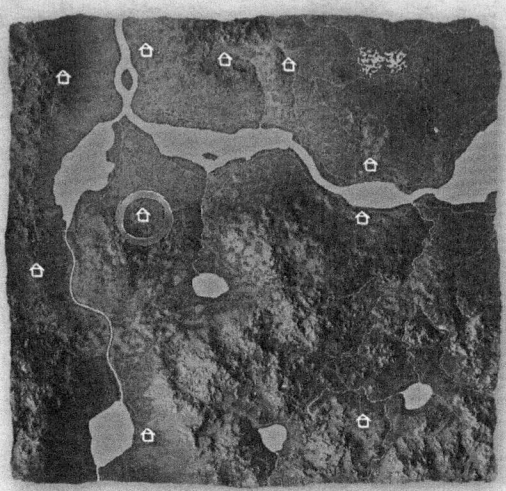

Description:

In the *Fold*, an animal breeder or even yourself can produce *Buckets of Milk* with goats, which you will need for baking. Per default, goats and sheep share a fold. Depending on how much milk you want to produce with goats and sheep, it could be a good idea to build separate folds for them, though. You can milk the animals by yourself too.

A dead adult goat provides you with 5 leather and 15–18 meat.

Sheep

Buy in:	Baranica
Male animal:	3900
Female animal:	3900
Young male animal:	1950
Young female animal:	1950
XP in farming:	2500
Average life span	12,5y

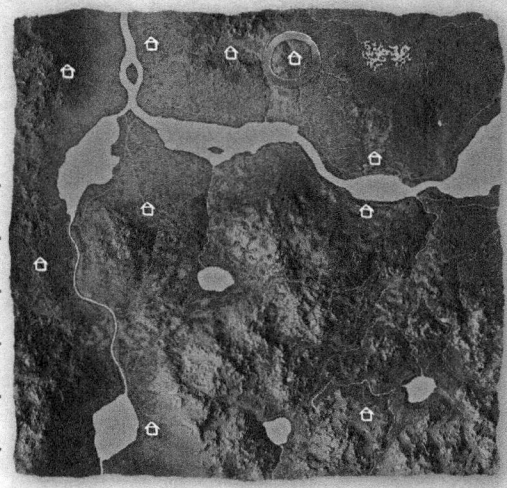

Description:

With sheep, you can produce *Wool*, which you can process into wool thread and wool fabric in the sewing hut.

If you slaughter a sheep, you receive 5 leather and 15-18 meat.

 **Pig**

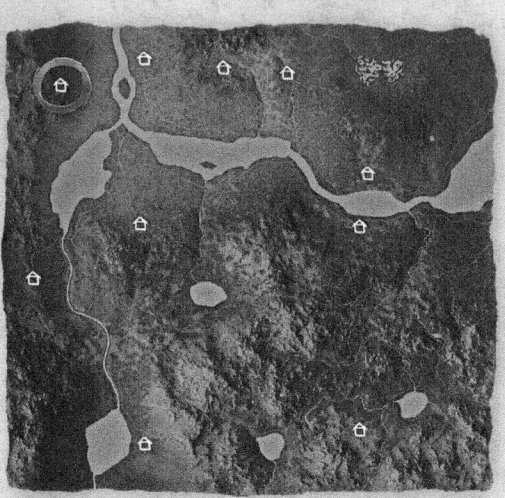

Buy in:	Rolnica
Male animal:	2250
Female animal:	2250
Young male animal:	1125
Young female animal:	1125
XP in farming:	250
Average life span	18.75y

Description:

Pigs produce *Manure*. You can use manure at the workbench of the barn to make fertiliser for fields. Pigs produce enough manure for large scale farming. You can also collect the manure from the ground by yourself.

A slaughtered pig gives you 5 leather and 20–22 meat.

Cattle

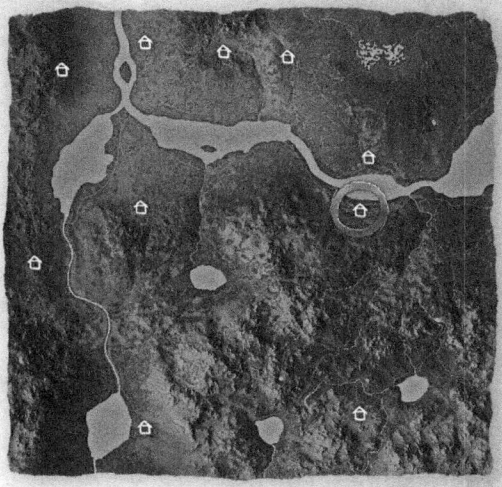

Buy in:	Gostovia
Male animal:	4500
Female animal:	4500
Young male animal:	2250
Young female animal:	2250
XP in farming:	3500
Average life span	22.5y

Description:

In the cowshed, animal breeders produce *Buckets of Milk* from cows. Cows are the second most expensive animals after horses and they only produce milk. The only other way to get milk is from goats or vendors.

A slaughtered cow provides 5-6 leather and 25 meat.

 **Donkey**

Buy in:	Tutki
Male animal:	3750
Female animal:	3750
Young male animal:	2625
Young female animal:	2625
XP in farming:	2000
Average life span	31.25y

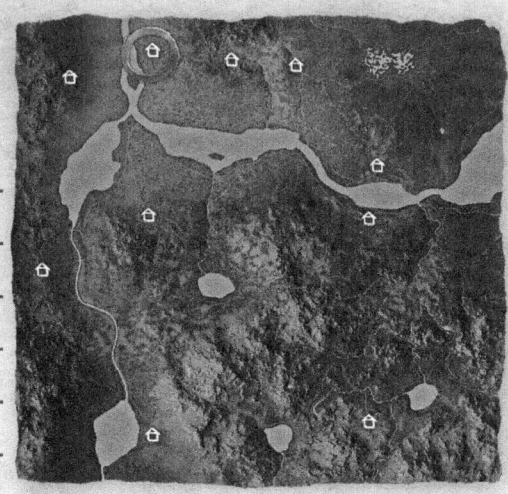

Description:

Donkeys live in the *Donkey Shelter.* An animal breeder is only for the automatic supply of the animals, nothing is produced.

Donkeys can be used as mounts with a saddle. Saddlebags increase their carrying capacity. Donkeys are slower than horses, but they can carry more. Also, a donkey shelter can be built much earlier than a stable.

Horseshoes reduce stamina consumption.

Horse

Buy in:	Hornica
Male animal:	10500
Female animal:	10500
Young male animal:	5250
Young female animal:	5250
XP in farming:	2000
Average life span	31.25y

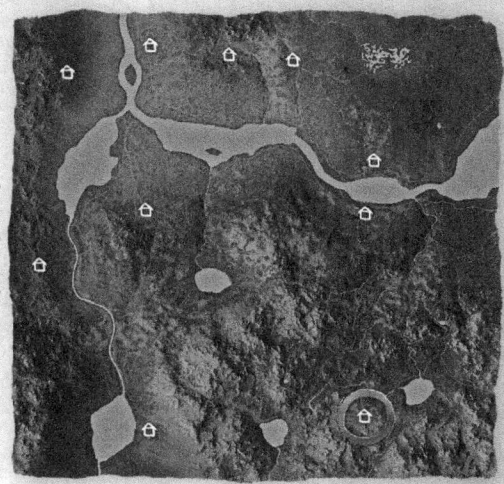

Description:

Horses live in the *Stable*. As well as with donkeys nothing can be produced with them. They serve purely as mounts, of which they are the fastest.

You can only get horses late in the game. They have a little less carrying capacity than donkeys, but you can also increase their carrying capacity with saddlebags. The main reason to own horses is to get faster from one place to another.

Horseshoes reduce stamina consumption.

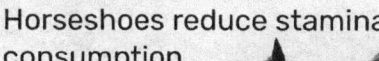

Apiary

The *Apiary* counts as animal husbandry, even though you don't have to buy animals for it. Building an apiary and assigning a villager to it is enough.

The apiarist will produce *Honeycombs* (containing honey), which you can eat or process into *Mead* at the *Tavern*. You can also get the honeycombs directly from the hives by yourself.

6.3   Mounts

You can equip horses and donkeys with saddles to ride them. Place the saddle in your inventory and look at the animal. Hold **E** / ⬤ / ✕ to saddle your mount.

To equip your mount with saddlebags or horseshoes, open your inventory. By holding down **X** / ✕ / ⬛, you can transfer an item from your inventory to the mounts inventory. Press **H** / Ⓡ / ⓡ③ to open the animal's inventory. Now you can equip your mount with horseshoes or saddlebags by selecting the object in the inventory.

If you are hit by a falling tree or your animal dies while you are riding, you will fall to the ground.

7 My Village

hirst for action is a good thing. Very useful. I still remember it well, when I was young and thought I could do everything alone. But that's a fallacy. Everyone needs an extended hand, to help when stumbling. No one can build a whole village by oneself.

Village! Over and over again people speak about villages although they actually mean hamlets. Three, four houses, some stables for the animals and they already think, they can call it a village. How delusional! It takes a lot more than that, I can tell you. Of course, houses are important, no doubt about it – a fire, a roof under which sometimes three generations of the same family live, a refuge against the wind and weather. And a home, to which you are always glad to return.

But a village? A village needs commerce, people who can produce many goods skilfully and rapidly, so that they can sell the excess, live from it and feed their family- and, last but not least, send wagon-loads over the mountain passes, to the bigger villages and even to cities. Where did you think the coins, we carry in our pouches, came from? Did you really think we mint our own gold and strike bracteates of silver? No, all the money circulating here, comes into our valley from elsewhere. Oh sure, we could trade. You know, I give you three pots of honey and you give me a new knife. Yes, this could go well for some time. Perhaps even longer. But there are goods we get from abroad, sometimes we have to pay mercenaries and, in addition to that, there are the taxes.

So, vendors and money, an important issue, but not the most important. The heart and soul of a village is the place where money gets spent. I don't know what you call it, where you come from. No matter if you call it bar, tavern, pub or alehouse – but without it, without an inn as a place to come together, a village is not a village. The ancient Romans and bards already knew: In taberna quando sumus, non curamus quid sit humus – and they were right!

Where wine and beer is poured, where the die are cast and singing voices sound drunkenly, where delicious meals are laid on the tables and where the folk occasionally indulge in dancing, is where the villages awakes to life.

Alas, how I would love to have the money of a lord and your youth again, just to rove the world one last time and stop off in every watering hole I pass through! Well, I have no shortage of coin – but the age, the age! Come on, get up and go to the chest in the corner there. Bring me my flute and the dice shaker. And while you're at it – on the shelf up there, there is a bottle of schnapps. Let's make a toast! Do you know a good song? Ha, let me think...

Under the lime tree on the heather, where we had shared a place of rest. Still you may find there, lovely together, flowers crushed and grass down-pressed. Beside the forest in the vale – Tándaradéi - Sweetly sang the nightingale...

7   My Village

7.1   Village Size & Growth

Number of Houses

The amount of buildings you can build depends on the number of completed chapter quests. With all of them completed, you can build 65 buildings.

You can adjust the building cap anytime in the settings under *Customize* (at 200% you can build 130 buildings after finishing the last chapter). You can't adjust this setting later!

Chapter	Name	Description	# Buildings
Chapter 1	Starting a new life	Hermitage	1
Chapter 2	A new beginning	Camp	5
Chapter 3	A survivalist	-	-
Chapter 4	Good morning my neighbors	Small Farm	10
Chapter 5	Into the wilderness	-	-
Chapter 6	A farm	Farm	15
Chapter 7	The resource fullness	Hamlet	25
Chapter 8	Starting a community	Settlement	35
Chapter 9	A big game	Village	45
Chapter 10	A newcomers	Town	55
Chapter 11	The dynasty continues	City	65

Villagers

The maximum number of villagers you can have depends on your *Dynasty Reputation*. The higher the value, the more villagers you can recruit. If you lose reputation while having the maximum number of villagers, don't worry: They won't move out. However, you will not be able to invite new villagers until you regain the lost reputation (plus the amount needed for the next villager)!

To increase your reputation, complete *Quests* and *Challenges, kill bandits* or *present toys to children*.

Let villagers marry

To each house you can assign a woman and a man respectively. The additional 1-2 beds are reserved for possible children.

If the age difference of the two occupants is less than 20 years, they become a couple after a few years and get children. The smaller the age difference, the faster the wedding!

As soon as a child is born, the mother will stop her current profession to take care of the baby for 2 years. After that, you can assign her to a profession again, until she possibly has another child.

> ### No such Thing as a Safe Job in the Middle Ages
> Be careful: the mother doesn't get her old job back automatically after her 2 years of motherhood!

Birth control

As a mother can't work for 2 years, you have various possibilities for birth control:

» Only assign either a woman or a man to a house. The drawback of this is that you need many houses.

» In the later game, assign a man and a woman with more than 20 years age difference.

» Let children who are of age continue living in their childhood house.

Growing up

When children turn 18, you can assign them to a different house from that of their parents and also marry them. If you continue to let them live with their parents, they can't get married or have children. Also, their mood will decrease!

Furthermore, you can send them to an apprenticeship and assign them a profession in the village after they have come of age.

Death

From their 60th birthday onwards, every inhabitant has a chance of dying. Therefore, you should have a thoroughly mixed age structure. If many villagers have the same age, several villagers might die within a few months and lead to a work capacity shortage!

Villager's Satisfaction

You can take a look at the satisfaction of your villagers in the *Management Display Screen* (*N* / ⊚ / Cr):

If the satisfaction of your inhabitants ever sink to -100%, they leave the village.

The following factors can increase their satisfaction:

> Bigger house made of good materials (stone) and limestone
> Enough water available
> Enough food available
> Enough firewood available
> Married
> Children younger than 18 in the house
> A profession with a high skill level
> Good events
> Fulfilled challenges for a good king

The following factors can decrease their satisfaction:

- Not having a house
- Missing water, food or firewood
- Damaged house
- No profession
- Children older than 18 in the house
- Bad events
- Fulfilled challenges for a bad king

Recruiting & Assigning a House!

Don't forget to assign a profession and a house to a newly recruited villager, so that his satisfaction doesn't decrease immediately!

7.2 Village Management

The key to village management is the *Management Display Screen* (*N* / ⊚ / ꭤ). Here you can control and arrange your villagers, fields, animals and needs.

People

In the people display screen ❶ you have an overview of all your villagers.

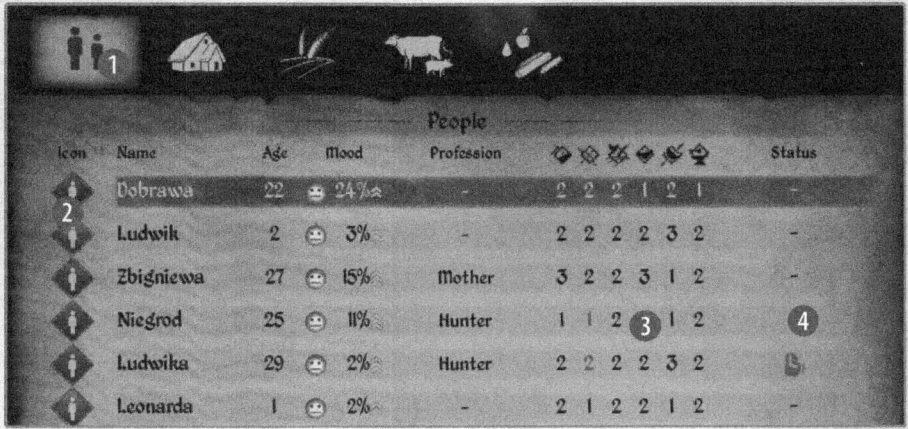

The icon ❷ indicates the persons identity:

Your wife		Man		Child
Your son		Woman		

In the many columns, you also see the villager's skills ❸. Green skills are those used in their current profession. Red icons in the status column ❹ stand for an impairment, like *No food* or *No water*. The green icon means *Pregnant*.

With a *double-click* / Ⓐ / ⊗ , you can open the detailed information of a person on the left. There, you can assign a new home or different profession.

Medieval Dynasty

Building display

In the building display ① you can see all your buildings:

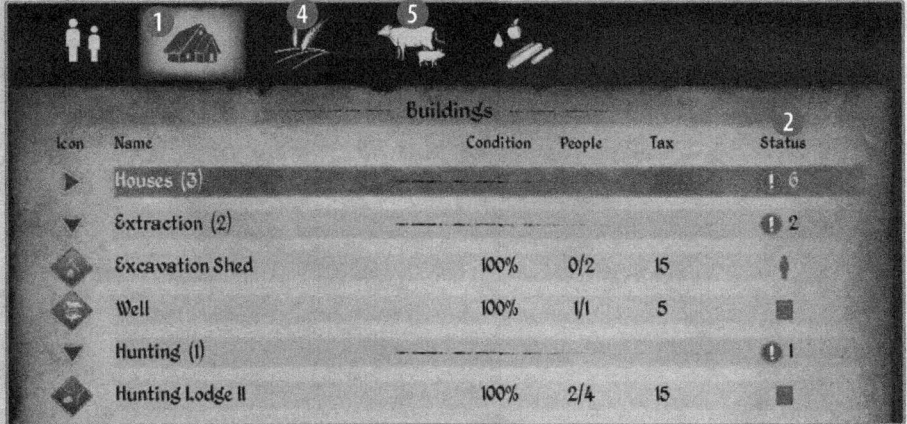

Next to the name, the condition, the employed inhabitants (people) and the tax prices (tax), you can see the status on the right side ②. Below, we show and explain icons of deficiencies:

Icon	Name	Description
❗	Group warning	There are warnings for this group of buildings.
✦	Damaged	The building is damaged.
👤	No worker	No worker is assigned to the building.
▤	No assignments	You didn't choose what the worker should produce. (management menu).
🔨	No tool	The required tool is missing.
⫶	No resources	The required materials for the production are missing.
🐖	No animal	The stable contains no animal and is empty.

By using the arrows, you can open or close the building groups (e.g., houses, extraction, hunting). Detailed information appears on the right side when you select a building.

Select the second icon at the top **3**, this will open the goods production & assignment window. Here, you can determine what the employed villagers should produce in the building.

You can find a more detailed description of producing goods in *Chapter 3 Building & Crafting*.

Crops & animals

On the left side of the management window, in the crops tabs **4** and animals tab **5** (see image on left page!), you can find an overview of your cultivated fields, orchards and your animal husbandry.

As in the previous overviews, the most interesting thing is the status column. Icons are also indicated in red here if there are problems.

By *double-clicking* (pressing Ⓐ/Ⓧ) on a field or animal you receive further information on the right side.

You can learn more about administrating fields and animals in *Chapter 6 Farming & Animal Husbandry*.

People's demand display

The last category of the management window is the *People's Demand Control* ❶:

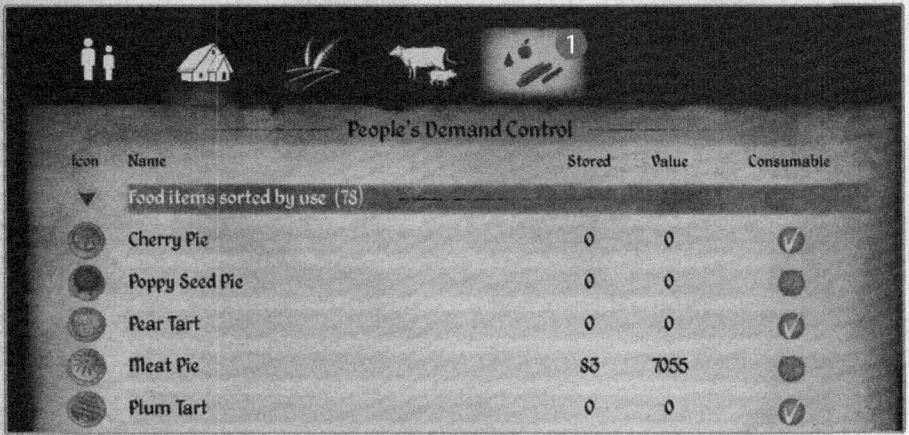

Here, you can see the amount of food, beverages and potential firewood you have in the resource and food storages.

You baked poppy seed pies just for a quest? You made a whole bunch or pear tarts but intend to sell them instead of using them as food for your villagers? By selecting the icon in the column *Consumable*, you can decide if your inhabitants should use the object or if they should ignore it. A red X means your inhabitants won't eat, drink or make a fire out of it.

In the same way you can protect products that you need for a different purpose.

Various Houses

On the following pages, we detail all the buildings you can build. For the residential houses, we will only show one variation of walls made out of plaited wattle, wood or stone.

Consider that the taxes increase in the game, the more buildings and inhabitants you have. The taxes indicated in this guide are the highest possible taxes that you have to pay in the last development stage of a village with about 55-65 buildings and the maximum amount of villagers.

At the beginning of the game, the taxes of your buildings are far lower. You can see them in the management display screen!

Simple Small House

Technology	-
Experience	-
Foundation price (Stone)	10 stones
Foundation price (Wood)	8 logs
Framing price	6 logs
Completion price	17 logs 66 sticks 32 straw
Chest capacity	50
Taxes per year	20
Max. inhabitants	3

Crafting stations

Cauldron	Production of soups, groats and other meals

Schemes you can buy

(none)

Description:

Houses can be built with 3 different wall types and roofs. In addition to that, the walls can also be plastered (see chapter 3).

As this house only has 3 beds, couples can only have one child. Later during the game it's perfectly suited for „birth control"

Simple House

Technology	Building
Experience	250
Foundation price (Stone)	12 stones
Foundation price (Wood)	10 logs
Framing price	10 logs
Completion price	22 logs 80 sticks 48 straw
Chest capacity	50
Taxes per year	40
Max. inhabitants	4

Crafting stations

Cauldron	Production of soups, groats and other meals

Schemes you can buy

Log Stool 500	Log Table 500	Log Bench 500
Window Curtain 500	Wooden Shelf 150	Hanging Rack 100

Description:

Houses can be built with 3 different wall types and roofs. In addition to that, the walls can be plastered (see chapter 3).

A bigger and more comfortable house with enough space for 2 children.

Medieval Dynasty

House

Technology	Building
Experience	1500
Foundation price (Stone)	14 stones
Foundation price (Wood)	12 logs
Framing price	12 log
Completion Price	24 logs 106 sticks 90 straw
Chest capacity	50
Taxes per year	60
Max. inhabitants	4

Crafting stations

Cauldron	Production of soups, groats and other meals

Schemes you can buy

Wooden Flowerpot 750	Decorated Wooden Door 1500	Braced Wooden Shutters 750
Wooden Double Shelf 750	Flower Himmeli 500	

Description:

Houses can be built with 3 different wall types and roofs. In addition to that, the walls can be plastered (see chapter 3).

Even bigger house than the two previous ones, this house is the "luxury flat". But there is, as in the simple house, only enough place for the parents and 2 children while taking up noticeably more space.

Woodshed I

Technology	Building
Experience	100
Foundation price	8 stones
Framing price	6 logs
Completion Price	2 logs 8 straw
Chest capacity	50
Taxes per year	20
Max. worker	1

Crafting stations

Carpenter's rack To chop logs up into planks and firewood

Schemes you can buy

Wattle Fence 250   Wattle Gate 300   Stone Flowerpot 250

Description:

Only in the woodshed can you make planks by yourself. Employed lumberjacks fell trees and produce sticks, logs, planks or firewood.

Woodshed II

Technology	Building
Experience	2500
Foundation price	8 stones
Framing price	6 logs
Completion Price	6 logs 6 planks
Chest capacity	100
Taxes per year	40
Max. worker	2

Crafting stations

Carpenter's rack To chop logs up into planks and firewood

Schemes you can buy

Wooden Stool 1000	Wooden Table 500	Wooden Bench 1500
Palisade 1000	Decorative Wooden Shutters 1000	Braced Wooden Double Shelf 1000
Hanging Lantern 500	Straw Wreath Himmeli 750	

Description:

The improved version of the woodshed, which can now occupy 2 lumberjacks.

Excavation Shed

Technology	Building
Experience	500
Foundation price	8 stones
Framing price	6 logs
Completion Price	20 logs 32 straw
Chest capacity	100
Taxes per year	60
Max. worker	2

Crafting stations

(none)

Schemes you can buy

Standing Torch 400	Wooden Fence 500	Wooden Gate 400
Clay Flowerpot 500	Batten Wooden Door 500	Rope Window Curtain 1000
Long Wooden Shelf 250		

Description:

Assigned workers mine stone, limestone, clay and straw.

 **Mine**

Technology	Building
Experience	5000
Foundation price	4 planks
Framing price	6 logs
Completion Price	10 logs 12 planks
Chest capacity	100
Taxes per year	180
Max. worker	6

Crafting stations

(none)

Schemes you can buy

Lantern 2000	Stone Fence 1500	Candlestick 1000
Flower Wreath Himmeli 1000		

Description:

A mine reinforces an already existing cave. This means that you can only build a mine at the entrance of one of the 5 caves in the valley. A mine offers the following advantages: The cave/mine is now illuminated, it has signposts inside, that indicate the exit and you can find iron ore inside. In comparison to an undeveloped cave, which offers only copper and tin ore, iron ore can also be found in the mine.

Miners bring you stones, salt, copper, tin and iron ore.

Well

Technology	Farming
Experience	50
Foundation price	4 logs
Framing price	4 logs
Completion Price	2 logs 16 straw
Chest capacity	50
Taxes per year	20
Max. worker	1

Crafting stations

Well Shaft   To fill containers with water

Schemes you can buy

(none)

Description:

A well secures the water supply even in barren areas.

A worker can fill buckets and waterskins with water automatically and store them in the food storage, thereby securing the water supply for your population.

Herbalist's Hut I

Technology	Survival
Experience	250
Foundation price	6 stones
Framing price	6 logs
Completion Price	6 logs 38 sticks 16 straw
Chest capacity	50
Taxes per year	20
Max. worker	1

Crafting stations

Herbalist's Table Production of various potions and poisoned ammunition

Schemes you can buy

Potion of Inst. Healing I 250	Potion of Healing I 250	Potion of Stamina 250
Potion of Saturation 250	Potion of Instant Cure 250	Poison 250
Potion of Weight 250	Potion of Temperature 250	Potion of Strength 250
Poisoned Stone Arrow 150	Poisoned Copper Arrow 150	Poisoned Bronze arrow 150
Poisoned Iron Arrow 150	Poisoned Wooden Bolt 150	Poisoned Copper Bolt 150
Poisoned Bronze Bolt 150	Poisoned Iron Bolt 150	Boar Fur Rog 100

Description:

A herbalist collects herbs, berries and mushrooms for you and can make potions and poisoned munitions. You can also make them by yourself at the crafting station of the building.

Herbalist's Hut II

Technology	Survival
Experience	2500
Foundation price	6 stones
Framing price	8 logs
Completion Price	40 logs 24 planks
Chest capacity	100
Taxes per year	40
Max. worker	2

Crafting stations

Herbalist's Table Production of various potions and poisoned ammunition

Schemes you can buy

Potion of Inst. Healing II 550	Potion of Healing II 550	Potion of Health 550
Potion of Satiety 550	Potion of Sobriety 550	Potion of Cure 550
Potion of Night Vision 550	Potion of Possibilities 550	Potion of Camouflage 550
Wolf Fur Rog 1000		

Description:

You can employ 2 herbalists in the improved herbalist's hut.

A herbalist collects herbs and mushrooms for you and can make potions. You can also make them yourself at the crafting station of the building.

Medieval Dynasty

Hunting Lodge I

Technology	Survival
Experience	50
Foundation price	8 stones
Framing price	8 logs
Completion Price	16 logs 66 sticks 32 straw
Chest capacity	50
Taxes per year	30
Max. worker	2

Crafting stations

Workbench   Production of bows, arrows and bolts

Drying Rack   Production of dried meat and dried fish meat

Schemes you can buy

Stone Spear 50	Bow 100	Stone Arrow 50
Bird Trap 80	Wooden Campfire 30	Badger Fur Rug 50

Description:

In the hunting lodge, you can make bows and arrows at the workbench.

The hired hunter only procures meat, leather, feathers and fur and can dry meat. He needs a knife as a tool in the resource storage or in the chest of the lodge!

Hunting Lodge II

Technology	Survival
Experience	1000
Foundation price	8 stones
Framing price	8 logs
Completion Price	41 logs 24 planks
Chest capacity	100
Taxes per year	60
Max. worker	4

Crafting stations

Workbench	Production of bows, arrows and bolts
Salting Barrel	Production of salted meat and salted fish meat
Drying Rack	Production of dried meat and dried fish meat

Schemes you can buy

Recurve Bow 1500	Medium Fishing Net 750	Moose Trophy 1000
Sheep Fur Rug 500		

Description:

In the improved hunting lodge, you can hire 4 hunters. Furthermore, there is now a salting barrel inside, which allows you to salt meat.

Fishing Hut I

Technology	Survival
Experience	500
Foundation price	4 logs 4 planks
Framing price	6 logs
Completion Price	13 logs 58 sticks 48 straw
Chest capacity	25
Taxes per year	20
Max. worker	1

Crafting stations

Workbench	Production of fish meat out of various fish sorts
Drying Rack	Production of dried meat and dried fish meat

Schemes you can buy

Longbow 500	Stone Campfire 150	Rat Trap 200
Small Fishing Net 250	Deer Trophy 500	Goat Fur Rug 200

Description:

A fisher supplies you with fish meat and can dry fish on the drying rack. Also, it can fillet your caught fish.

You can make fish meat out of caught fish (roach, perch and pike) by yourself and also dry meat and fish.

Fishing Hut II

Technology	Survival
Experience	5000
Foundation price	4 logs 4 planks
Framing price	6 logs
Completion Price	38 logs 36 planks
Chest capacity	50
Taxes per year	40
Max. worker	2

Crafting stations

Workbench	Production of fish meat out of various fish sorts
Salting Barrel	Production of salted meat and salted fish meat
Drying Rack	Production of dried meat and dried fish meat

Schemes you can buy

Big Fishing Net 1500	Wisent Trophy 1500	Bear fur Rug 1500

Description:

Here, there is enough room for two fishers and there is an additional salting barrel to process it into salted fish meat.

Barn I

Technology	Farming
Experience	10
Foundation price (Stone)	12 stones
Foundation price (Wood)	8 logs
Framing price	10 logs
Completion Price	14 logs 64 sticks 48 straw
Chest capacity	250
Taxes per year	60
Max. worker	4

Crafting stations

Workbench	Production of animal feed, fertilizer, daub and poppy seeds
Quern	Production of flour
Threshing Floor	To thresh crops

Schemes you can buy

Flour 50	Daub 50

Description:

Three for one! In the barn three crafting stations allow you to further process crops (threshing and milling) and also let you produce daub, animal feed and fertilizer. These chores are done by barn workers.

Farmers can also be assigned here, who take over the care, sowing and harvesting of fields and looking after orchards.

Barn II

Technology	Farming
Experience	1500
Foundation price (Stone)	12 stones
Foundation price (Wood)	8 logs
Framing price	10 logs
Completion Price	41 logs 48 straw
Chest capacity	500
Taxes per year	90
Max. worker	6

Crafting stations

Workbench	Production of animal feed, fertilizer, daub and poppy seeds
Quern	Production of flour
Threshing Floor	To thresh crops

Schemes you can buy

(none)

Description:

You can have 2 further workers in the barn II (6 in total). You can employ each worker as a farmer or barn worker depending on your needs.

Barn III

Technology	Farming
Experience	8000
Foundation price (Stone)	12 stones
Foundation price (Wood)	8 logs
Framing price	10 logs
Completion Price	17 logs 36 planks 64 stones
Chest capacity	1000
Taxes per year	120
Max. worker	8

Crafting stations

Workbench	Production of animal feed, fertilizer, daub and poppy seeds
Quern	Production of flour
Threshing Floor	To thresh crops

Schemes you can buy

(none)

Description:

The last development stage of the barn allows you to employ 8 workers and is much more durable than its predecessors.

Henhouse

Technology	Farming
Experience	100
Foundation price	6 stones
Framing price	4 logs
Completion Price	8 logs 30 sticks 24 straw
Chest capacity	50
Taxes per year	30
Max. worker	1

Crafting stations

(none)

Schemes you can buy

Animal feed 50

Description:

In the henhouse, there is space for 10 chickens and one animal breeder. They produce eggs and feathers.

Pigsty

Technology	Farming
Experience	250
Foundation price	8 stones
Framing price	6 logs
Completion Price	12 logs 54 sticks 12 straw
Chest capacity	50
Taxes per year	40
Max. worker	1

Crafting stations

(none)

Schemes you can buy

(none)

Description:

5 pigs and one animal breeder can occupy a pigsty and industriously produce assiduously manure there.

Goose House

Technology	Farming
Experience	500
Foundation price	6 stones
Framing price	4 logs
Completion Price	9 logs 54 sticks 16 straw
Chest capacity	50
Taxes per year	60
Max. worker	1

Crafting stations

(none)

Schemes you can buy

(none)

Description:

The goose house holds 10 geese and one animal breeder and supplies you with eggs and feathers.

Fold

Technology	Farming
Experience	2500
Foundation price	10 stones
Framing price	6 logs
Completion Price	13 logs 62 sticks 32 straw
Chest capacity	50
Taxes per year	80
Max. worker	1

Crafting stations

(none)

Schemes you can buy

(none)

Description:

A fold can contain up to 12 goats or sheep (or a mix of both!). If an animal breeder is assigned to the fold, goats produce milk and sheep wool.

You can milk and shear the goats by yourself.

Buckets for milk and shearing scissors have to be available in the resource storage, though!

Cowshed

Technology	Farming
Experience	3500
Foundation price	10 stones
Framing price	8 logs
Completion Price	18 logs 104 sticks 32 straw
Chest capacity	50
Taxes per year	100
Max. worker	1

Crafting stations

(none)

Schemes you can buy

(none)

Description:

A cowshed has space for 8 cows. With an animal breeder, they produce milk (bucket with milk). The buckets have to be provided in the resource storage!

You can also milk the cows by yourself.

Stable

Technology	Farming
Experience	2000
Foundation price	12 stones
Framing price	10 logs
Completion Price	32 logs 48 straw 5 planks
Chest capacity	100
Taxes per year	100
Max. worker	1

Crafting stations

(none)

Schemes you can buy

(none)

Description:

A stable can be the home of up 4 horses. Since Version 1.4, donkeys can no longer be assigned to the stable. If you have assigned donkeys to the stable in your old savegame, they will remain in the stable.

The animal breeder simply feeds the animals and does not produce anything.

Apiary

Technology	Farming
Experience	5000
Foundation price	6 stones
Framing price	4 logs
Completion Price	2 logs 14 straw 3 planks
Chest capacity	50
Taxes per year	40
Max. worker	1

Crafting stations

(none)

Schemes you can buy

(none)

Description:

The apiary produces honeycombs if an apiarist is assigned to it.
In the tavern, you can make tasty mead out of the honeycombs.
You don't have to buy bees, they will appear as soon as the build-
ing is constructed.

Workshop I

Technology	Production
Experience	10
Foundation price (Stone)	10 stones
Foundation price (Wood)	8 logs
Framing price	8 logs
Completion Price	4 logs 32 straw
Chest capacity	100
Taxes per year	40
Max. worker	1

Crafting stations

Workbench　　Production of wooden everyday objects

Schemes you can buy

Small Wicker Basket 50	Wooden Bowl 100	Wooden Cup 100
Wooden Plate 100	Wooden Ladle 50	Wooden Spoon 50
Bucket 100	Wooden Vial 50	

Description:

You or craftsmen assigned by you can make wooden objects at the workbench.

Workshop II

Technology	Production
Experience	250
Foundation price (Stone)	10 stones
Foundation price (Wood)	8 logs
Framing price	8 logs
Completion Price	32 logs 24 planks
Chest capacity	200
Taxes per year	80
Max. worker	2

Crafting stations

Workbench	Production of wooden everyday objects
Pottery Wheel	Production of clay everyday objects

Schemes you can buy

Torch 250	Medium Wicker Basket 200	Clay Bowl 300
Clay Bottle 300	Clay Jug 300	Clay Cup 300
Clay Mug 300	Clay Vial 300	Cay Vase 300
Clay vase with Chicory 10	Clay Vase with Daisy 10	Clay Vase with Dandelion 10
Clay Vase with Dandelion 10	Clay Vase with Henbane 10	Clay Vase with St. John's Wort 10
Clay Vase with Thistle 10		

Description:

In the improved workshop, you find another crafting station, the pottery wheel. With it, you can produce all clay items (jug, bottle, bowl).

Additionally, you can employ a second craftsman.

Workshop III

Technology	Production
Experience	3500
Foundation price (Stone)	10 stones
Foundation price (Wood)	8 logs
Framing price	8 logs
Completion Price	20 logs 56 stones 48 planks
Chest capacity	300
Taxes per year	120
Max. worker	2

Crafting stations

Workbench	Production of wooden everyday objects
Pottery Wheel	Production of clay everyday objects

Schemes you can buy

Large Wicker Basket 350	Wicker Crate 500	Wooden Wheel 500
Beer Bottle 450	Mead Bottle 450	Wine Bottle 450

Description:

Even though the workshop III doesn't have more space or crafting stations, it's now completely closed and made from solid stone.

Smithy I

Technology	Production
Experience	50
Foundation price (Stone)	8 stones
Framing price	8 logs
Completion Price	7 logs 24 sticks 32 straw
Chest capacity	100
Taxes per year	60
Max. worker	1

Crafting stations

Anvil	Production of all metal weapons and tools
Forge	To produce copper, tin, bronze and iron bars out of ores
Workbench	Production of stone and wooden tools and weapons

Schemes you can buy

Stone Sickle 100	Wooden Bolt 50	Cudgel 50
Copper Bolt 100	Copper Hammer 100	Copper Axe 150
Copper Hoe 150	Copper Shovel 100	Copper Sickle 150
Copper Knife 150	Copper Arrow 100	Copper Spear 150

Description:

Melting ores and producing weapons is the job of the blacksmith. An employed blacksmith will need a hammer, so he can work.

Smithy II

Technology	Production
Experience	500
Foundation price (Stone)	8 stones
Foundation price (Wood)	8 logs
Framing price	8 logs
Completion Price	22 logs 24 planks
Chest capacity	200
Taxes per year	100
Max. worker	2

Crafting stations

Anvil	Production of all metal weapons and tools
Forge	To produce copper, tin, bronze and iron bars out of ores
Workbench	Production of stone and wooden tools and weapons

Schemes you can buy

Bronze Hammer 200	Bronze Axe 250	Bronze Pickaxe 350
Bronze Hoe 250	Bronze Shovel 200	Bronze Sickle 250
Bronze Knife 250	Bronze Scythe 350	Bronze Arrow 200
Bronze Bolt 200	Bronze Spear 250	Bronze Shearing Scissors 200
Wooden Crossbow 250		

Description:

You can employ a second villager in the smithy II.

Smithy III

Technology	Production
Experience	5000
Foundation price (Stone)	8 stones
Foundation price (Wood)	8 logs
Framing price	8 logs
Completion Price	7 logs 18 stones 48 planks
Chest capacity	300
Taxes per year	140
Max. worker	2

Crafting stations

Anvil	Production of all metal weapons and tools
Forge	To produce copper, tin, bronze and iron bars out of ores
Workbench	Production of stone and wooden tools and weapons

Schemes you can buy

Iron Knife 500	Iron Hoe 500	Iron Shovel400
Iron Spear 500	Iron Crossbow 1500	Iron Bolt 500
Iron Scythe 750	Iron Axe 500	Iron Pickaxe 750
Iron Hammer 400	Iron Arrow 250	Iron Sickle 500
Iron Horseshoes 200	Iron Shearing Scissors 400	Iron Spiked Cudgel 500

Description:

The smithy III is now made from fireproof stone (no, this does not mean that the other smithies can burn down!)

Sewing Hut I

Technology	Production
Experience	100
Foundation price	8 stones
Framing price	8 logs
Completion Price	9 logs 32 sticks 40 straw
Chest capacity	50
Taxes per year	60
Max. worker	1

Crafting stations

Tailoring Table	Production of various clothes and other things
Spinning Wheel	Production of linen and wool thread
Loom	Production of linen and wool fabric

Schemes you can buy

Linen Thread 50	Bag 50	Linen Fabric 50
Simple Linen Shirt 200	Linen Shirt 250	Trousers 200
Trousers with Cuffs 250	Fur Capelet 300	Coif 100
Straw hat 50	Flat Straw Hat 100	Shoes 200
Simple Shoes	Fur Shoes 300	Thick Leather Gloves 200
Small Pouch 200	Simple Small Backpack 400	Saddle 500
Small Saddlebag 500		

Description:

The sewing hut possesses everything to craft fabrics and clothes.

Sewing Hut II

Technology	Production
Experience	750
Foundation price	8 stones
Framing price	8 logs
Completion Price	69 logs 24 planks
Chest capacity	100
Taxes per year	100
Max. worker	1

Crafting stations

Tailoring Table	Production of various clothes and other things
Spinning Wheel	Production of linen and wool thread
Loom	Production of linen and wool fabric

Schemes you can buy

Wool Thread 250	Simple Tunic 500	Hose 300
Wool Fabric 250	Short Sleeve Tunic 500	Tunic 700
Joined Hose 400	Hat 200	Cap 150
Cap with Coif 200	Hood 400	Fur Hood 600
Fur Boots 500	Boots 500	Pouch 600
Simple Backpack 1000	Saddlebag 1000	

Description:

The sewing hut II has been built weatherproof and is more durable than its predecessor.

Sewing Hut III

Technology	Production
Experience	7500
Foundation price	8 stones
Framing price	8 logs
Completion Price	17 logs 57 stones 48 planks
Chest capacity	200
Taxes per year	140
Max. worker	2

Crafting stations

Tailoring Table	Production of various clothes and other things
Spinning Wheel	Production of linen and wool thread
Loom	Production of linen and wool fabric

Schemes you can buy

Felt Vest 1000	Quilted Vest 1500	Hat with Lapels 300
Felt Hat 400	Bag Hat 500	Long Hood 500
Long Fur Hood 700	Fancy Shoes 400	Noble Shoes 500
Noble Boots 600	Large Pouch 1000	Simple Large Backpack 2000
Large Saddlebag 2000		

Description:

It is now possible to employ two seamstresses in the sewing hut III.

Kitchen I

Technology	Production
Experience	25
Foundation price	8 stones
Framing price	8 logs
Completion Price	10 logs 34 sticks 32 straw
Chest capacity	200
Taxes per year	40
Max. worker	1

Crafting stations

Stove	Production of bread, pies and tarts
Cauldron	Production of groats, soups and other meals
Stone Grate	Roasting meat and fish meat

Schemes you can buy

Porridge 50	Gruel 50	Potage 100
Stew 100	Soup 150	Meat with Gravy 150
Mushroom Soup 25	Scrambled Eggs 100	Quark 100

Description:

All prepared meals are cooked in the kitchen. Soups in the cauldron, bread and cakes in the stove and grilled meat on the stone grate. The ingredients and any dishes only need to be available in the appropriate storage and the cook can get started.

Kitchen II

Technology	Production
Experience	1500
Foundation price	8 stones
Framing price	8 logs
Completion Price	38 logs 48 planks
Chest capacity	200
Taxes per year	80
Max. worker	2

Crafting stations

Stove	Production of bread, pies and tarts
Cauldron	Production of groats, soups and other meals
Stone Grate	Roasting meat and fish meat

Schemes you can buy

Flatbread 150	Flatbread with Onion 200	Oat Roll 250
Rye Bread 250	Wheat Bread 300	Multigrain Bread 350
White Bread 350	Wheat Roll 300	Porridge with Berries 100
Scrambled eggs with Mushroom 150	Vegetable Soup 200	Cheese 300

Description:

For a bigger village, you can employ two cooks in the kitchen II.

Tavern

Technology	Production
Experience	10000
Foundation price (Stone)	10 stones
Foundation price (Wood)	10 logs
Framing price	10 logs
Completion Price	64 logs 96 planks
Chest capacity	300
Taxes per year	140
Max. worker	2

Crafting stations

Brewing Station	Production of ale, beer and mead
Juice Press	Production of various juices
Wine Barrel	Production of various wines

Schemes you can buy

Fish Tart 350	Fruit Tart 400	Meat Tart 450
Meat Pie 450	Fruit Pie 450	Pear Tart 450
Plum Tart 450	Poppy Seed Pie 500	Cherry Pie 500
Porridge with Apple 200	Berry Juice 350	Apple Juice 400
Cherry Juice 400	Pear Juice 400	Plum Juice 400
Berry Wine 450	Apple Wine 550	Cherry Wine 500
Pear Wine 550	Plum Wine 600	Mead 500
Oat Ale 400	Oat Beer 450	Rye Beer 450
Wheat Beer 500		

Description: All beverages are produced here.

Market Stall

Technology	Production
Experience	2500
Foundation price	4 logs 4 planks
Framing price	4 logs
Completion Price	4 planks 8 linen
Chest capacity	none
Taxes per year	60
Max. worker	1

Crafting stations

(none)

Schemes you can buy

(none)

Description:

An assigned vendor sells the goods you have chosen. Open the management display to see the ware group of the market stall and change the wares to be sold.

There are market stalls for tools (and weapons), clothes, material, food and herbs (and potions). Depending on the wares you sell, the appearance of the market stall changes.

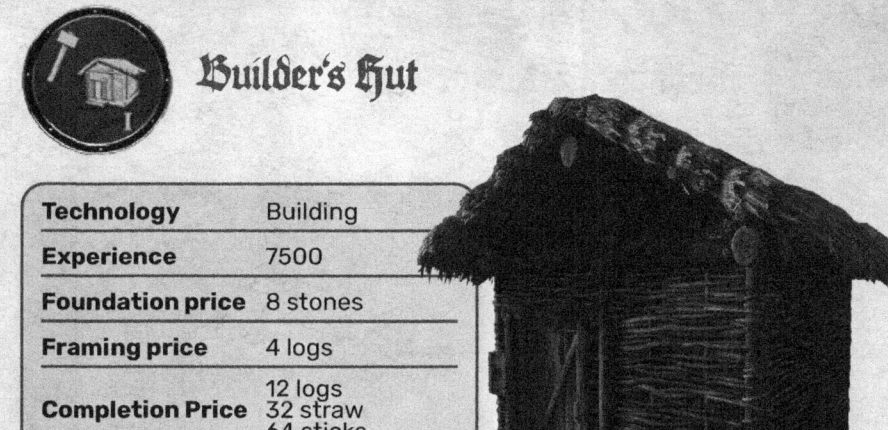

Builder's Hut

Technology	Building
Experience	7500
Foundation price	8 stones
Framing price	4 logs
Completion Price	12 logs 32 straw 64 sticks
Chest capacity	100
Taxes per year	100
Max. worker	1

Crafting stations

(none)

Schemes you can buy

Large Flower Himmeli 1500

Description:

A builder in the builder's hut doesn't produce anything. But he repairs the damaged buildings in the village by himself, provided the required materials are stored in the resource storage.

Resource Storage I

Technology	Building
Experience	50
Foundation price (Stone)	12 stones
Foundation price (Wood)	10 logs
Framing price	10 logs
Completion Price	17 logs 48 straw 64 sticks
Chest capacity	1000
Taxes per year	60
Max. worker	none

Crafting stations

(none)

Schemes you can buy

Sitting Stump 250	Stick Fence 150	Stick Gate 200

Description:

In the resource storage, you store all items, tools, resources and materials except for food.

The villagers and workers take the materials and tools they need (firewood for the inhabitants, a hammer and ores for the blacksmith, seeds, a scythe and fertiliser for the farmer etc...) by themselves.

Resource Storage II

Technology	Building
Experience	1000
Foundation price (Stone)	12 stones
Foundation price (Wood)	10 logs
Framing price	10 logs
Completion Price	82 logs 30 planks
Chest capacity	2000
Taxes per year	120
Max. worker	-

Crafting stations

(none)

Schemes you can buy

Log Fence 800	Braced Wooden Door 1000	Wooden Shutters 500
Braced Wooden Shelf 500	Double Hanging Rack 500	Straw Himmeli 250
Log Gate 800		

Description:

The resource storage II has more storage capacity.

If you have more than one resource storage, they share their inventory and storage capacity. In one resource storage, you have access to the complete inventory of all the resource storages.

Resource Storage III

Technology	Building
Experience	10000
Foundation price (Stone)	12 stones
Foundation price (Wood)	10 logs
Framing price	10 logs
Completion Price	34 logs 60 planks 98 stones
Chest capacity	4000
Taxes per year	180
Max. worker	-

Crafting stations

(none)

Schemes you can buy

Large Flower Wreath Himmeli 2000

Description:

In the biggest resource storage, you have a storage capacity of 4000kg. Furthermore, it is also the most solid, due to the stone walls!

 Food Storage I

Technology	Farming
Experience	5
Foundation price (Stone)	14 stones
Foundation price (Wood)	8 logs
Framing price	10 logs
Completion Price	35 logs 32 straw 62 sticks
Chest capacity	500
Taxes per year	40
Max. worker	-

Crafting stations

(none)

Schemes you can buy

(none)

Description:

In the food storage, all drinks, mushrooms, cooked dishes and all raw, salted and dried meat as well as fish are stored. Spoiled food is also stored in it.

All food storage increase the durability of the food stored in them by four times the player's inventory.

Medieval Dynasty

Food Storage II

Technology	Farming
Experience	1000
Foundation price (Stone)	14 stones
Foundation price (Wood)	8 logs
Framing price	10 logs
Completion Price	63 logs 24 planks
Chest capacity	1000
Taxes per year	80
Max. worker	-

Crafting stations

(none)

Schemes you can buy

(none)

Description:

Like the resource storages, the food storages share a common inventory and combine their capacity so that you can get to the content of all of them from any food storage.

 ## Food Storage III

Technology	Farming
Experience	6500
Foundation price (Stone)	14 stones
Foundation price (Wood)	8 logs
Framing price	10 logs
Completion Price	34 logs 24 planks 64 stones
Chest capacity	2000
Taxes per year	120
Max. worker	-

Crafting stations

(none)

Schemes you can buy

(none)

Description:

The most solid food storage with the biggest storage capacity.

Windmill

Technology	Farming
Experience	10000
Foundation price	4 logs 10 planks
Framing price	8 logs
Completion Price	70 logs 10 planks
Chest capacity	2000
Taxes per year	120
Max. worker	1

Crafting stations

Quern   Production of flour

Schemes you can buy

(none)

Description:

The long awaited mill! Gives your village extra charm. There, as well as at the quern in the barn, you can grind flour. The windmill can produce twice the quantity of flour than the barn with the same amount of grains.

Donkey Shelter

Technology	Farming
Experience	250
Foundation price	8 stones
Framing price	6 logs
Completion Price	16 planks 4 logs 32 straw
Chest capacity	6 planks
Taxes per year	50
Max. worker	1

Crafting stations

(none)

Schemes you can buy

(none)

Description:

The donkeys have finally got their own home, the donkey shelter.
It can accommodate 4 donkeys. Here, as well, an animal breeder
produces nothing and serves merely the welfare of the animals.

8 Marriage & Offspring

You don't look like you're married – because if you did, what would you be doing here all alone? Would you not be with your woman and your children? Ah, no need to be ashamed, I got married late too – and never regretted it! Yes, it has to be well considered, not only with the heart, but also with reason, when you take the plunge over the fire.

Ah, I forgot, you probably don't know what I'm talking about. It is a tradition of the people here, an ancient custom, the monks and abbots don't like to see. The polite name it pagan and the grim name it blasphemous and outrageous – but old customs disappear as slowly as old gods. You have to understand, back in the day, and that's not that long ago, marriage was a completely different thing here in the land of the Slaves. When two people found each other, they would jump over the fire together during spring in front of all their gathered friends, relatives and the whole village!

But this wasn't the marriage yet, not the union forever. The girl took on the boy for a trial year, to make sure he was up to scratch. If not, she broke the union – yes, that's exactly what does not please the bigots. And if she was carrying a child under her heart, it wasn't a disgrace, nor reason for shame – on the contrary! Young women with children were more in demand than virgins, because they had shown their womb was fertile and that they are selective.

Rumor has it that this still exists in some even more remote valleys and in the East, where the Rus live. But times have changed here – for the better or for the worse is not for me to judge. Many of the ancient customs had their right of existence, if you ask me, and we should not shove them aside thoughtlessly.

Either way, here, we get married in accordance with the new custom and that means – no trial period, they who bind themselves, are bound for their whole life! According to this, you have to make an effort to conquer the heart of your chosen one and often enough also the approval of her father. A good reputation and a perfect status with the most important people of the village are the first steps! If the old blacksmith praises your strength, the big farmer your hard work and the reeve your honesty, you will stand out. And naturally, you must have something to offer to your woman! A poor blighter without a roof over his head will not be the first choice of one of the beautiful girls of the valley – let's be honest, not even the second or the third.

A sturdy abode that can resist the autumn storms, good skills with bow and arrow, a plot of fertile and fecund land that you can farm, and enough clinking copper coins and silver pieces in your purse – and on top of that, naturally, a healthy appearance. Being healthy and strong is more important here than wearing the hair according to the latest city fashions. And grow a beard! Like mine, but not grey!

8 Marriage & Children

8.1 Courting a Woman

As a dynasty lasts beyond a single generation one of the most important goals in the game is having an heir. This challenge you cannot master all alone, of course. You will need a wife, and you probably do not want it to be just anyone.

But let's start at the beginning. Potential marriage candidates you can find in NPC villages and even in your own village. All recruitable or recruited female characters are also potential marriage candidates. With two important restrictions:

> She has to be single.

> The age difference between you cannot be greater than 10 years.

Regular villagers already living in NPC villages and unique NPCs that you can meet during Family Quests cannot be married.

Inviting your love interest to your village as an inhabitant first makes sure that she will not move on before you can ask for her hand. Just be careful to not put her into a house with another suitable male character. She might choose him over you.

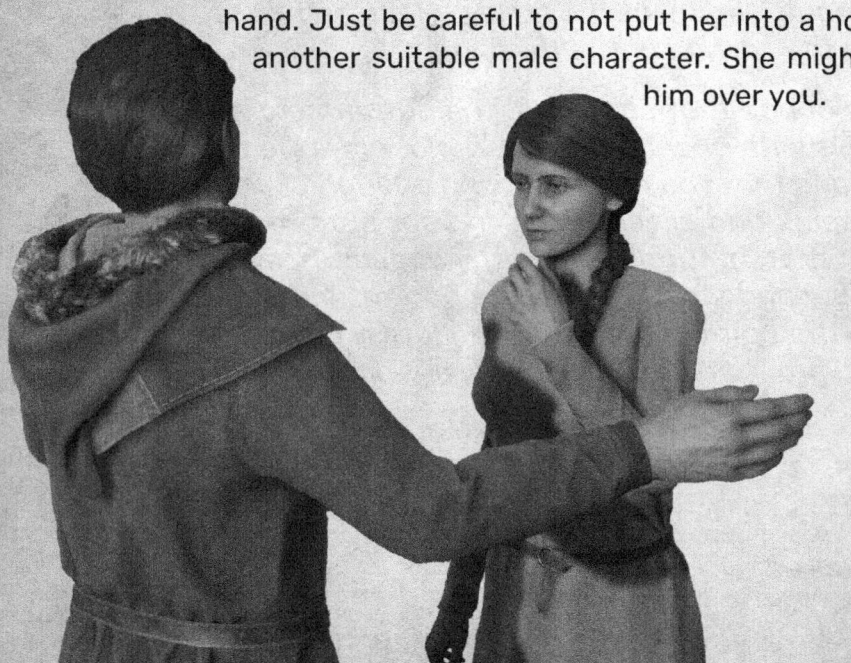

Women Personalities

As the village leader you are free to choose your wife, marry after careful consideration or simply for love. Just do not wait too long, remember that all men must die, and you want your heir to be at least 18 years old when the inevitable happens (any season after age 60 can be your last).

In the game you will meet different women with one of four distinct personality types. Dialogues and a woman's reaction to flirting and gifts differ depending on those personality types.

Free Spirit

Unrestrained and creative. She drinks you under the table and longs for the adventures of the wide world. Crude jokes make her tell you another. If only the world would not expect her to be chained to a hearth above all else.

Positive topics	Compliments, pick-up lines, morning sun, honesty, almost all animals, her voice, her eyes, divorce, cleverness
Neutral topics	Medicine, love, hard work, her clothes, her sensibility, butterflies
Negative topics	The king's castle, being a mother, death, dull world, the king's future, athletic physique
Best gifts	Glass beads (500), flute (500), dried dates (750), dried figs (750), Madeira wine (1000)

Busy Bee

Hardworking and homebound. She is a master of all things practical and her approach is always hands on. Focus on what is in front of you, don't waste time daydreaming. If only the rest of the world were as efficient as her.

Positive topics	Hard work, honesty, cleverness, almost all animals, divorce, being a mother, athletic physique, medicine, jokes
Neutral topics	The king's castle, birds, pick-up lines, her voice, her smell
Negative topics	Love, death, morning sun, compliments, her clothes, her eyes, dull world, how demanding she is, the king's future
Best gifts	Coverlet (500), thimble (500), glass bottle (750), needle case (750), pouch of spices (1000)

Romantic

Loving and longing. She is a gentle soul who follows her heart and yearns to open its doors to you and the child you might have. Gallant and noble is the man of her dreams. If only the world could be more like a romantic ballad.

Positive topics	The king's future, the king's castle, honesty, love, birds and pigs, being a mother, her eyes, her voice, compliments, death, dull world, morning sun, her clothes
Neutral topics	Her smell, jokes, medicine, bad things, cleverness
Negative topics	Almost all animals, divorce, hard work, pick-up lines, athletic physique
Best gifts	Perfume (500), hand fan (500), silk shawl (750), kaptorga (1000)

Snob

Prideful and self-centred. She knows her worth, and a crown would fit her head far better than a plough her hand. Without a doubt she is the fairest of them all. If only the world would let her rule over more than a flock of chickens.

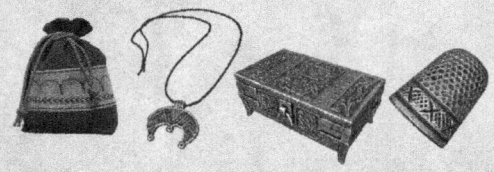

Positive topics	The king's future, the king's castle, cleverness, compliments, her voice, her eyes, her smell, birds, morning sun, honesty, death
Neutral topics	Love, divorce, being a mother, medicine, dull world, bad things, almost all animals, hard work
Negative topics	Jokes, bees, pick up lines, athletic physique, her clothes
Best gifts	Amber necklace (500), silver earrings (500), golden ring (750), lunula (750), Jewellery box (1000)

Gaining Affection

Knowing a woman's personality is key to winning her heart. The Empathy skill perk (Diplomacy) will help you with that and display her personality for you after a first initial conversation and gaining at least 20% affection. The personality of strangers will not be shown right from the start!

Conveniently with one look at the initial window of the dialogue menu you will also always know how much affection she has for you and how your choices affect it, no perk required. Strangers always start with 0% affection. The percentage increases or decreases depending on your romantic dialogue choices and gifts. Do not confuse mood with affection!

No woman will agree to marriage or, later, to a child, if her affection for you is not high enough.

Affection is not only important to win a woman's heart, but also to keep it. If you make no effort to keep your *wife's affection up* after marriage, it will decrease and she will eventually leave you. If your heir is not yet 18 years old, she can take him with her.

His own affection for you will decide if he stays or goes with her. To prevent a family tragedy like this altogether, talk to her, help her with Family Quests and, of course, gifts are a girl's best friend as well.

Like any other villager, your wife and son will also be affected by mood changes depending on their living circumstances. And just like any other villager they may leave your village if it drops to minus 100. Affection however is unique to potential marriage candidates and your family.

In the following let's take a more in-depth look at conversation and gifts.

Conversation

Women in the game have one additional dialogue category: the Romance option. If they are already married or not interested for other reasons, they will politely tell you so, not offer any more flirtatious dialogues and point you to better candidates.

The first 2-4 dialogue options in the Romantic category will help you understand a woman's personality and reveal it if you have the Empathy skill perk. They will also always increase her affection.

So, don't worry, you cannot scare her off with a bad first impression. Unless you are too dirty or too drunk. In which case she will refuse to speak to you until you have washed and/or sobered up.

Medieval life is busy and after a short conversation (2-4 questions or comments) the woman will tell you that she has to think about what you said. Return the next day if you wish to continue talking to her.

Now, keep the woman's personality in mind and try to select dialogue choices that match it. For example, the Busy Bee is a hard worker. She will love to be praised for it, but dislike conversations about vain trivialities and court intrigues. The Snob, on the other hand, will be the exact opposite.

Two abilities in Diplomacy will help you to handle romantic conversations with ease:

Level 1 – *Romeo*: Depending on the level of this ability you increase your conversation partner's affection by 10%, 30% or 50% more when flirting.

Level 2 – *Empathy*: If you increase the level of affection a woman has to you to at least 20%, you will see her personality next to the % indication.

Gifts

Everybody loves gifts, especially when picked with consideration. This is no different for the women of Medieval Dynasty.

Every season a vendor for *exotic goods* arrives in a different tavern of the valley. That tavern can be one of the NPC villages or one in your own village. The vendor icon can be seen on the compass when you are nearby, and all NPCs can tell you in which village to find him or her if asked.

Exotic goods are the only gifts that can be given to women. They are expensive (usually between 750 and 1500 coins), but when given during a romantic conversation they can significantly increase your love interest's or wife's affection.

Make sure to choose a gift that fits her personality for the best result. Our list above will help you with that if you are unsure.

Children love gifts as well. You can buy gifts like toy swords and ragdolls from regular vendors in the valley (e.g. smiths and seam-stresses). Those gifts will increase your heir's affection, but they can also be given to random children in your village. They will keep those gifts and you will see them happily play with them.

Everybody will only accept *one gift per season*.

8.2   𝔚𝔦𝔣𝔢 & ℭ𝔥𝔦𝔩𝔡

While you can flirt with several women at the same time, you can only marry one of them.

You will be able to remarry and even have a new child with a new wife after your old wife leaves you or you banish her from your village, but let us hope that it will not come to this.

Once your love interest reaches 90% affection there will be a chance for her to agree to your marriage proposal, a dialogue choice among the romance options. At 100% she will always accept.

The wedding takes place right away and will be shown in an illustrated cut scene. Afterwards your wife will move into your house.

If she wasn't an inhabitant of your village before, you can now also assign a workplace to her. If she already has one, she will keep it and only change house to be with you.

Remember! Over time your wife's affection will decrease. Keep your love alive by talking to her, successfully completing her Family Quests, and giving her a gift from time to time. If you fail to do so and her affection drops to 0%, or her mood to -100, she will leave you and potentially take your underage child with her. Her dialogue will reflect her growing unhappiness. If she leaves you due to a loss of affection, not mood, there is a chance that your son may stay in the village when she leaves, unless you have neglected him as well.

Help from your Wife

Marriage is a give and take. Of course, your wife will not just make demands, but also help you out in turn. Not only will she work in your village like any other, she can also assist you with the management:

» You can ask her for details about the village and she informs you of existing problems (e.g., damaged houses or insufficient food supplies).

» You can ask her to pay the taxes (or possibly debts) to the castellan. This way you won't have to take the trip to Gostovia yourself.

» You can ask her to inform the herald of the king that all the required resources for a challenge are in the resource or food storage. This also spares you a trip.

And she keeps an eye on your personal needs:

» If you are dirty, she will wash you.

» If you are wearing inappropriate clothes for the season, she will remind you to change them.

» If you are drunk, she will call you out.

» If you are hungry or thirsty, she may give you something to eat or drink.

» If you are hurt, she will heal you.

Your wife can not reset your skill points. For this you will need a Potion of Possibilities.

Your Heir

So far, the player character's child will always be a single child and it will be a son.

At any point after your marriage, you can ask your wife if she feels ready to become a mother. As long as the basic necessities (you have a house, food, water, firewood) are given and she has enough affection for you, she will agree to having a child with you and ask you to come to her in the evening (7 P.M.).

At the given time find her and talk to her once more to seal the deal. There will be no cut scene, only a discrete black screen, but afterwards your wife will be pregnant.

Three seasons later (equal to 9 months with three "days" as months per season) your wife will give birth to your son. Here a cut scene will illustrate the event and you can pick a name from a list of possibilities.

Like other female villagers your wife will not work for 2 years, watching over your son.

Your son's skills will be influenced by your own and those of your wife, but they can be improved via apprenticeship. As is the case for all other children born in your village he will also gain additional skill points per age stage.

Like your wife your son will occasionally have quests for you, his dialogue depends on his personality, and he will happily accept a gift per season or offer you a small gift himself.

Once you start playing as your heir, you will be rewarded with additional points to spent in his skill tree, depending on his affection level on his 18th birthday. The higher his affection for you as a child, the more bonus points you will receive once he becomes an adult. If you receive one bonus point, you will receive one for each skill, of course. The highest bonus of 4 points is hard to reach!

Once he turns 14 you can also assign your heir as an apprentice to a workplace, like any other villager.

At 18 you can assign him to his own house and workplace. If he shares a house with a female villager, he may even marry her and have children before you take over playing as him. If you wish to play him during

these important events in his life, be careful who you let him move in with!

18 years old is also the time when you can switch from playing his father to playing as him. This can happen after your current player character's death, be it due to age (at some point after 60), an accident, or if you decide to let your current player character retire.

Children's Skills

The skills of all children born in your village are determined by a formula based on the average of their parents, which may be adjusted some more in future game updates.

What you can rely on is that each age stage increases all skills of the child. If you observe the little ones over the years, you can tell when they have grown up some more: they look very different. Or you keep these numbers in mind: Infant (0 - 1), Toddler (2 - 6), Child (7 - 13) and Teenager (14 - 17).

So, three times the skills of the child will increase automatically before it reaches adulthood.

Skills can be further increased by sending the youngster to train with older workers (starting age 14) and, of course, once he/she joins your actual workforce at age 18.

All in all, raising your own villagers comes at the cost of their mothers not working for two years, but it will reward you with highly skilled workers that you cannot find elsewhere and that do not need to be recruited. The latter also means that you do not have to meet a certain threshold of Dynasty Reputation points to be able to invite them. Remember, that threshold increases which each adult villager already living in your village.

The number of children is only limited by the number of free beds in their parents' house. Even older villagers may still have new children after the old ones have moved out from home.

Heir Personalities

Like your wife your son can have one of four distinct types that shape your interactions with him.

During the first years of his life, he will take after your wife.

At 7 years old a special quest, the *Ceremonial Haircutting*, finally allows you to influence his personality. Your decisions here will define his personality for the future.

Possible personality types are:

» **Daredevil**: Analogous to the Free Spirit wife. He is carefree and untamed, and only his cleverness keeps him out of more serious trouble. His enthusiasm is easily roused but vanes just as quickly.

» **Simple Hearted**: Analogous to the Busy Bee wife. He is enduring, patient and obedient. His loyalty towards his father whom he admires is genuine and without question, as is his love for hard work.

» **Daydreamer**: Analogous to the Romantic wife. He is sensitive and shy, a tender and careful boy. His big heart has room for all creatures big and small, just not for hard work and boring daily chores.

» **Lone Wolf**: Analogous to the Snob. He is quiet and withdrawn, even distant and harsh at times. His days are spent planning and preparing for a future in which he will be strong and self-sufficient.

Ceremonial Haircutting

At your heir's 7th birthday an age-old family ritual marking the first step into adulthood will take place: the Ceremonial Haircutting.

Until this point the young boy has spent most of his time with his mother, now the time has come for the father to assume a bigger role in his life. Not only will his hair be cut, you will also go on an adventure together.

So far, your wife's personality has influenced that of your son. Now your choices will decide if and how it will change for the future.

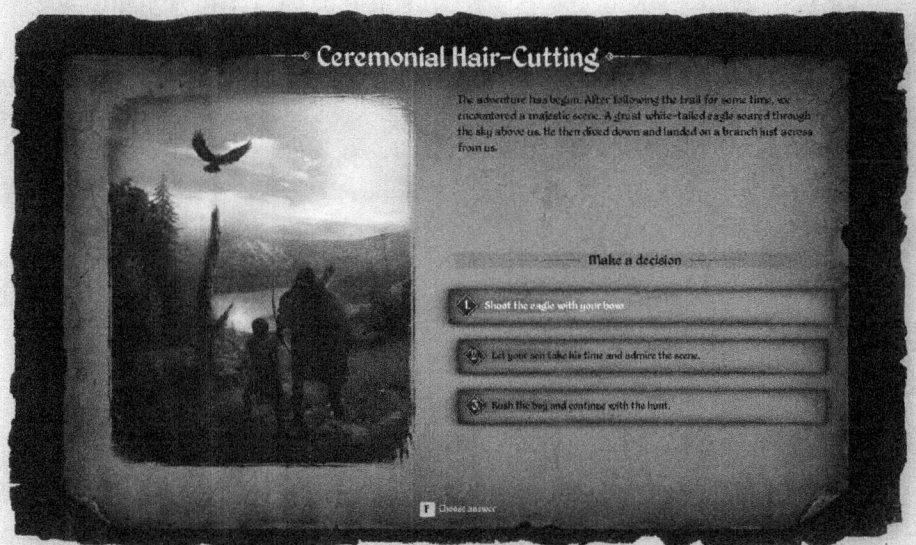

While we would recommend letting your intuition guide you here, this is the definite result that your choices will have:

Daredevil	Simple Hearted	Daydreamer	Lone Wolf
Cut your son's hair.	Let him do the cutting.	Cut your son's hair.	Let him do the cutting.
Encourage him to have fun on the hunt.	Educate your son about the awaiting dangers.	Scare him into obedience.	Don't say anything.
Let your son take his time and admire the scene.	Rush the boy and continue with the hunt.	Let your son take his time and admire the scene.	Shoot the eagle with your bow.
Stop him from eating and explain his mistake.	Stop him from eating and explain his mistake.	Stop him from eating and yell at him for not being careful.	Let him eat the mushrooms and learn from his carelessness.
Scare the boarlet away. It should get back to its mother.	You cannot ignore nature's gifts. Kill the boarlet for meat.	Let your son come closer and pet the boarlet.	Small targets are good practice. Kill the boarlet for sport.
Tell your son to look away and end the deer's misery.	End the deer's misery, but instruct the boy to watch.	Leave it be and let nature do its thing.	Make the boy finish off the deer himself.
Letting somebody steal from you is a sign of weakness. Proceed onwards.	Letting somebody steal from you is a sign of weakness. Proceed onwards.	It may be too dangerous to continue with a child. It's best to go back. [By choosing this option you skip the next choice and go straight to the end.]	It may be too dangerous to continue with a child. It's best to go back. [By choosing this option you skip the next choice and go straight to the end.]
Create a diversion and run. Not honourable, but effective.	Attack, disarm and let the bandit go. We're not the same as them.	Co-operate calmly and do as he asks. It's not worth risking your life.	Attack, disarm and kill the bandit. Survival of the fittest.

Your son will now have one of the following personalities.

Daredevil	Simple Hearted	Daydreamer	Lone Wolf
As soon as we returned home, he left my side and started telling all of the adults about our hunt. He didn't hold himself back from boasting about his bravery and valour. He's got a lot to learn, but I like his attitude. Confident, open and sociable. I'm sure he'll do well in life.	When we came back home, he didn't leave my side until the end of the day. I've noticed how closely he observed my every move. There's nothing more satisfying to a father. I hope he'll never lose his focus, ambition and determination. I really admire that about him.	As soon as we came back home, he left my side and ran to his peers. I overheard him mentioning his mother. He can't be blamed, their bond was naturally strong. Nevertheless, I'm proud of the way he handled himself today. He was a little out of his depth, but remained calm, compassionate and true to his own nature. I love him very much.	As soon as we came back home, he left my side and went about his own thing. I've noticed that he likes solitude. At first, I was a bit worried about it, but I'm not anymore. Not after today. What I see now is a young man, who knows his worth and doesn't need anyone's approval apart from his own. I wish him all the best.

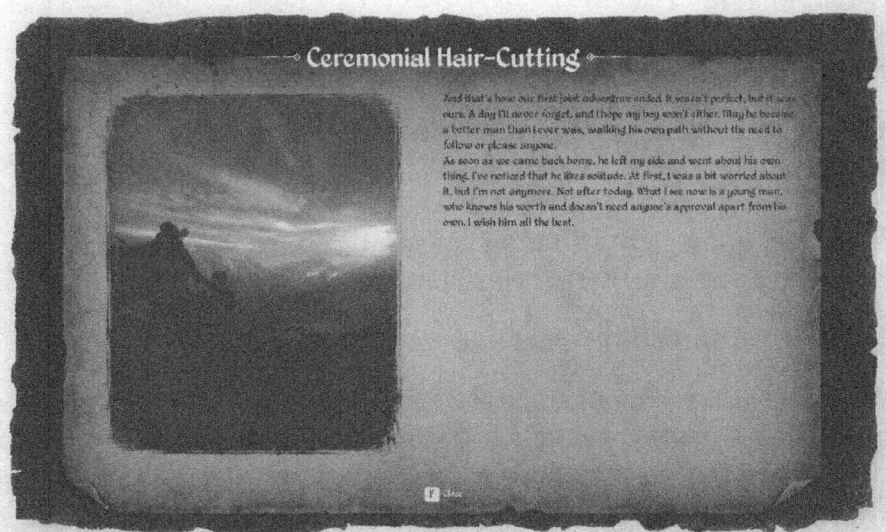

— Ceremonial Hair-Cutting —

And that's how our first joint adventure ended. It wasn't perfect, but it was ours. A day I'll never forget, and I hope my boy won't either. May he become a better man than I ever was, walking his own path without the need to follow or please anyone.

As soon as we came back home, he left my side and went about his own thing. I've noticed that he likes solitude. At first, I was a bit worried about it, but I'm not anymore. Not after today. What I see now is a young man, who knows his worth and doesn't need anyone's approval apart from his own. I wish him all the best.

Family Quests

Other than the Ceremonial Haircutting the "Heir Update" has added several new family related quests to the game.

Those Family Quests will start as soon as you marry. Afterwards pregnancy and each age stage of your heir will bring about new quests from him or your wife.

Those stages are: After Marriage (any time), Pregnancy (0-3 seasons after conception), Infant (0 - 1), Toddler (2 - 6), Child (7 - 13) and Teenager (14 - 17).

The dialogues will be different depending on your wife's and son's personality.

Completing these quests will increase your Dynasty Reputation as well as your wife's and son's affection. (Remember that your son's affection will result in bonus points that you can spend in his skill tree once he reaches adulthood!)

You will also gain special rewards and meet unique NPCs who can be recruited for your village. Those will have their own name, look, and background story, and they will be highly skilled.

The women cannot be married.

If a Family Quest is not accepted or ignored, it will appear again for the next generation. If it is completed or failed, it will not appear again in the same playthrough.

The following NPCs can only be met and recruited during Family Quests:

Unique NPCs

Name	Quest	Highly skilled in
Amerigo	The Stranger	Diplomacy
Nimrod	Lost	Hunting
Astrid	Maiden of the North	Extraction
Roland	The Master Angler	Survival
Nikola	Mother of Inventions	Production
Georgiana	The Dirty Deed	Farming

9 Tips & Tricks

'm glad you want to stay in the valley with us – yes, I would have offered you one of my old huts, up there at the edge of the forest; But if you insist to stand on your own two feet, why not! You have more coins than I did then and I will give you some advice for free every time you knock on my door. Here, have another flagon, the apple brandy really came out excellent this year. It warms up from the inside, ha-ha! So, as I said, just drop in if you have questions. I'm always glad to have a visitor – well, I should say, almost always.

If you play your cards well, you will have an extraordinary, happy and fulfilled life. We do not adapt to the noise of the cities. The war is far away from our valley and we pray to the new god and to the old ones that it stays that way. We are subordinates of the the seasons, and you will learn what that means. Work hard during spring, conscientiously in summer and gratefully in the first weeks of autumn. Believe you me, the soil will repay you generously. You will get some time, during autumn and winter to extend and to embellish your house, learn some craftsman abilities.

You will meet people, some shy some open hearted, some good and some perhaps less so – but many friendships will come to be and hearts will open to you. Perhaps you will already find a woman during spring, perhaps only in many years – but you can find all you desire here. Apart from furniture upholstered with velvet or golden crowns, ha-ha!

But if you take good care of your money, let it increase uprightly and honestly, then there will be enough of it left after years of work to employ others to your service. Oh, don't get me wrong, a competent wife and hard-working kids are already a big help, but with some strong arms at your service you'll proceed faster. And there are enough young boys and girls in the valley, who will help you build your own hamlet and even perhaps a whole village, with an own tavern, into which, I will limp, even in my older days, to drink one or two mugs to your health. And to mine!

Your future lays in this valley my friend – so, what are you waiting for? Here, I'll pack you a fresh loaf of bread, my daughter just made this morning and...

...what is that?

Can you hear that too?

No, I don't know, it sounds like...

... a call for help! No, calls for help! An assault!

It must come from the mountain; The wind carries the shouts down here. Bandits? What? Bandits here in our valley? NO! Not with me!

Come, take my old hunting spear in the corner there, and the oil lamp! Where did I – ah, here it is! My crossbow and I still have enough bolts. Well, don't tremble like that, I'll show you how we defend ourselves in the valley, no matter if you're old or young! Let's get to the mountain and let's fight!

9 Tips & Tricks

In this last chapter, we want to sum up the most important tips for the game. You have probably already seen some of them in the other chapters, but we wanted to make a compact list of all of them here.

9.1 Keeping an Overview

Collecting

While collecting, grass and foliage disturb your search for many things. During the winter, there is no disturbing grass and you can see many small and bigger things on the ground faster (for example, left behind items or buried treasures).

Furthermore, you can set the *Foliage* on *Low* in the graphics settings. This makes searching a lot easier.

Using the inspector mode

As already mentioned several times: in your skills, learn the *stage 2 ability Survival Sense* in *Survival* and the *stage 2 ability Tracker* in *Hunting*. Then, you can track down just about every animal, herb, mushroom and item by holding down the *Alt* / LB / L1 key.

Overview of villagers and houses

In the *Management Display Screen*, you can see information about all villagers, houses, animals and fields. Look at their *Status Column* in the right window from time to time. If there are red icons there, something is wrong and you should take a closer look. A *double-click* / Ⓐ / Ⓧ opens the *Details Overview* on the left side!

Furthermore, you have a *Map* on the bottom right of the management window. If you select a person or a house in the left list, you see their current position on the map! Fields and houses can be given names as well. That makes it easier to find them.

You can also ask your wife. She tells you if something is not working as it should in your village!

Better sight through night vision

The *Potion of Night Vision* works like an amplifier for residual light. It also offers you a better sight during cloudy days, in dark forests or caves - not only at night! Use a *Torch* in addition, to increase its effects (especially in caves!)

Map filters

On the Map (*M* / ⊚ / Ⓒⓡ), use the various filters (*A* /◄╋/◄◗ & *D* /╋▶ /◗▶ to switch!) to find quests or your buildings.

Change your perspective

Your field of view is too small? In the settings, you can increase the visible angle (*Field of View*) from 90° up to 110°.

9.2 The Best Building Tips

Build where you want!

You can build everywhere you like and where there are fairly flat surfaces. You can gain space for your houses by felling trees and removing the stumps with a shovel. There is not really a bad place to build your village. Here are a few tips:

» For beginners, it's helpful to build near Gostovia, as you often have to go there in the beginning.

» Having reed close by only reduces material gathering time in the beginning of the game (straw for roofs).

» Having a cave not too far away is practical for the ore mining.

» Flat surfaces for buildings and to create fields.

How should I build?

Residential houses and production buildings should be built close to one another, ensuring short traveling distances:

› Build a barn next to fields. On the opposite side, build the houses of the farmers.

› Only relevant for animation and flair: woodshed close to the forest and hunting lodge not far from game.

Orchards are simple

Orchards don't require much effort, you only have to harvest during summer and don't need to take care of the trees in any other way. Furthermore, occasional fruit trees are a nice decoration. So, plant fruit trees as early as possible. Even if you don't need fruit, you can always sell it.

Map with good building places

On the following map, we marked some places well suited for the construction of villages. Mostly near a water source, a clay deposit, most of them with a cave not too far away and with some nice scenic places offering enough space:

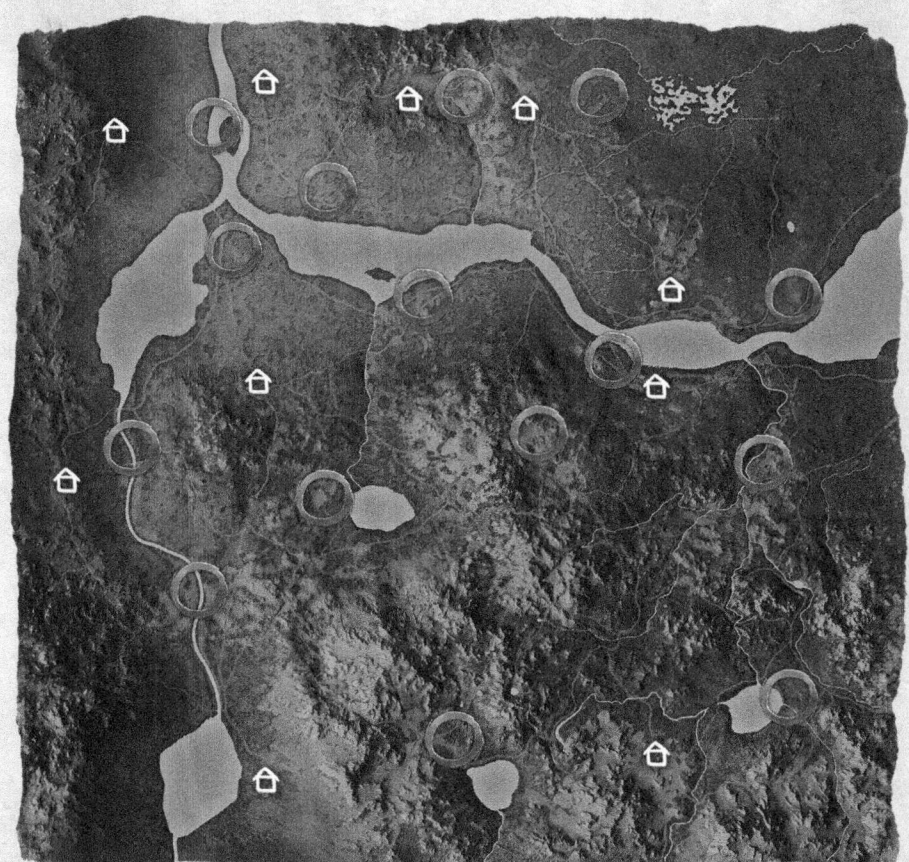

Decoration - building with objects

You can throw any object on the ground. Look at it and whilst holding down *E* / Ⓐ / ⊗, pull it to the desired position. Like this, you can, e.g., build a bridge out of planks or logs over a small stream or build decorations.

Decorate your village with accessories like buckets, wooden wheels or tools on tables etc.

If you want to use food as decoration, you need to enable *Stop Dropped Items from Spoiling* in the Gameplay Settings. Food in your inventory and in chests will still rot.

Carrying too much?

You want to build several buildings but already reached your carrying limit with only the logs for their carcass?

Collect the materials beforehand and throw them on the ground near the building site. Then, take as much as you can carry and start building. For new supplies, you only have to pick up the materials nearby from the ground. Doing so prevents interrupting long walks to get further supplies.

This method is also useful if you want to collect many stones and sticks to sell stone knives at the beginning. Collect the materials and put them ,e.g., in the middle of the road, where you can easily find them. Like this, you can collect a big amount of material without being overburdened and slowly, before you begin crafting the knives!

Houses' quality

In the long run, only houses made of stone and plastered with limestone are worthwhile. The wattle and wooden walls quickly become damaged. You always have to repair them, even with a builder's hut, which can be really annoying. Furthermore, you save heating costs and the villagers are more satisfied in better houses.

Annoying farm animals?

Animals escaping from their stables and blocking your village's road again? (We don't even want to think about cow dung right in front of the entrance of the tavern!)

Don't build the stables facing towards your (main) road. Better build the entrance on the opposite side. You can even block the directions, they should not go, with fences. You close an opening in the fence with a gate. This keeps the animals inside and lets you and villagers through.

Then, most of the animals won't loaf around your road anymore and only one or two chickens on it makes for a picturesque image.

Medieval Dynasty

9.3 Investing or Saving Money

Quick earning from the start?

» Fulfill the story quests from Dobroniega (inn-keeper in Gostovia and wife of Uniegost – rye delivery from Rolnica) and you will gain 500 coins, definitely a good beginning.

» At night, steal objects in Gostovia (don't get caught!) and sell them in a different village. A good opportunity for dishonest characters.

» Stone knives! We said it multiple times: gather sticks and stones and craft stone knives. You can sell each for 15 coins. You can craft 40 stone knives quite fast (consider the *Collecting Tip* at the beginning of this chapter and the tip *Carrying too much*?!) and whoosh, 600 further coins.

Money later during the game

Overturned carts, buried treasures, abandoned camps and forgotten items offer you the possibility to earn some coins on the side. Either you find coins or you can sell the items. Think about it: the place where you find the items always stay the same but they randomly appear at every change of a season!

If you have some villagers producing something, you will soon have one or the other excess. Sell it, you should get enough money from it!

You have an enormous surplus? Build a market stall as soon as you can, assign a villager to it and sell your wares. You don't need to do anything and you earn money every day, as long as you have wares to sell!

Saving money?

At a change of a season, you should have saved 500 to 1500 coins, so that you have enough money available for a possible event.

Try to always pay the taxes during spring, if not, you lose reputation. You lose it faster than you gain it!

Investing money?

Are you (like me, the author) an impatient player? Then it is more than profitable to spend your hard-earned money for metal weapons and tools at the beginning of the game. They accelerate collecting, building and make hunting a lot easier!

If you are patient, you can make do with a stone axe, stone knives and wooden spears and can save your money for other things (this sentence sent shivers down my spine).

You will have to buy your first seeds and fertiliser (unless the 20 onion seeds you receive from one of Alwin's quest are enough and that you wait patiently for food to rot, to make fertiliser in the barn).

Some events allow you to gain a lot of experience in one of your skills in exchange for coins. These coins are a good investment, since you would have to work much longer to gain the experience, than to gain the coins!

9.4 Fighting & Hunting

Bandits

The best way to kill bandits is by using bows and crossbows. Why have a dangerous close combat fight, stab or hit them dozens of time if a single headshot is enough?

Beware of archers and crossbowmen. Most of the time, they are the bandits, who stay behind. You must kill them first!

Hunting animals

Use good weapons (e.g., longbows or metal arrows) and creep up on the animals by holding the *Ctrl* / Ⓡ / ⓡ₃ key. A headshot will kill most of the animals.

Aggressive animals stare at you and make warning noises, as soon as they notice you. This is the perfect moment for a headshot!

Big wisents and bears are challenging when only equipped with a bow. The hardy hunter uses 2-3 bronze or iron spears and kills them with one or two headshots. (The third spear is only to play it safe – you never know!)

What? You can't afford metal weapons, because you're at the beginning of the game? Take a closer look at tip 9.3!

9.5 Further Tips

A quick keybind overview

Key	Effect	Key	Effect
①-⓪/ ⇕ / ⬧	Selection of the tool/ weapon	ⓡ / Ⓨ / △	Equip/ Unequip current tool/ weapon
Ⓦ Ⓐ Ⓢ Ⓓ / Ⓛ / Ⓛ③	Movement	⇆ / ◉ / Cr	Open last window
Ⓠ/ RB / R1	Creation menu	① / ◉ / Cr	Inventory
Ⓔ / Ⓐ / ⓧ	Interact	Ⓚ / ◉ / Cr	Skill Management
Ⓕ/ ⓧ / ▢	Torch	Ⓙ / ◉ / Cr	Journal
Ⓟ/ ↔ / ⬌	Change 1st Person View / 3rd Person View	Ⓜ / ◉ / Cr	Map
Ⓗ / ✛ / ⬇	Hide/ Unhide HUD	Ⓝ / ◉ / Cr	Management Display Screen
Alt / LB / L1	Inspector Mode (hold)	Ⓣ / ◉ / Cr	Technology Display Screen
Strg / Ⓡ / R3	Creep up (hold)	Ⓛ / ◉ / Cr	Knowledge Display Screen

Don't forget, indicated at the bottom right corner of the screen, you have the usable keys and commands, when using a tool or a weapon!

Medieval Dynasty

Which crops should you plant?

Basically, plant the crops you need for further productions. Early in the game, combining cabbage and rye is a good way to maximally optimize your fields during a year:

Spring: harvest rye/ sow cabbage

Summer: harvest cabbage/ sow cabbage

Autumn: harvest cabbage/ sow rye

Winter: rye is growing and repeat this process the following year

This way you can harvest your fields 3 times a year. With cabbage and meat, you can produce potage you can sell or feed to your inhabitants and from rye you receive straw and rye grains, you can process to flour.

Our cabbage field is harvested during autumn by a farmer, while a second one's already ploughing, fertilizing and sowing rye:

Rat traps

With rat traps you will achieve success everywhere and the extra ration of meat is always welcome! With the hunting skill *Trapping Master* you can also build additional rat traps!

Use the quick saving option! (PC only)

Our last but nevertheless quite important tip: use the quick save and quick load feature.

F5 = quick save

F9 = quick load

With these commands, you can save the game any time before important decisions, construction projects or adventures and if something doesn't work out, you can load the saved game again, without having to open the saving screen display!

Index

Index

Online Interactive Map

Our online map of Medieval Dynasty shows you all the spots where you can find game, farm animals, broken down carts, buried treasures, lost items, bandit camps and even more.

You find the interactive map on:

www.bildnerverlag.de/en/medieval-dynasty

Made in United States
North Haven, CT
15 November 2022

26753499R00213